MW00654921

HANDBOOK OF
CHORAL MUSIC SELECTION,
SCORE PREPARATION
AND
WRITING

HANDBOOK OF CHORAL MUSIC SELECTION, SCORE PREPARATION AND WRITING

Kenneth E. Miller

Parker Publishing Company, Inc.   West Nyack, New York

© 1979 by

PARKER PUBLISHING COMPANY, INC.

West Nyack, NY

*All rights reserved. No part of this book
may be reproduced in any form or by
any means without permission in writing
from the publisher.*

Library of Congress Cataloging in Publication Data

Miller, Kenneth E
   Handbook of choral music selection, score preparation and writing.

   Includes bibliography and index.
   Appendices (p.   -   ): I. Compliance with the
copyright law.—II. Publishers of choral music.—
III. A selected list of choral music.
   1. Choral music.
ML1500.M6   784'.1   79-14010
ISBN 0-13-372532-4

Printed in the United States of America

To
Rose Marie, Ann and Kay
Each made an enormous contribution.

THIS BOOK IS MADE POSSIBLE IN PART BY SUPPORT FROM THE
UNIVERSITY OF MISSOURI-ST. LOUIS

A Word About
The Practical Value
Of This Book

Musicians have discussed virtually every topic pertinent to the field of choral music with me, and those discussions have been on many levels. But, of all the topics explored, three have emerged as most in need of increased attention and understanding. Those three topics are: (1) choral music selection, (2) score preparation and (3) writing, and they will be discussed in this book.

The careful selection of music is one of the most important steps to be taken toward achieving a successful choral music program. After you have chosen the music, you will benefit from careful and comprehensive score preparation. And, you may also find it necessary to write original music, or to make arrangements, in order to have music available which best suits your particular singers.

This book will help you with actual, everyday problems. If you teach in a small situation you will find helpful suggestions, as will those of you who teach in more established programs. Many points will be directed to you who conduct young choirs, but matters will be applicable as well to working with mature concert organizations. Practical matters will be discussed in each chapter.

You, as a teacher of choral music, spend much time choosing music to be used. And your preferred plan should be not only to select music for performance, but also to select music for the interest and musical growth of your singers. Generally, choral conductors are improving the selection of music used. But we all will agree, no doubt, that there is much room for improvement in making good music available, particularly to middle school and high school students. Some of the more important topics included in this book are:

1. The Need to Know Your Singers
2. Criteria in Selecting Choral Music
3. Maintaining the Choral Library
4. Score Preparation and the Choral Conductor

5. The Suitability of a Text
6. The Training of the Conductor
7. Musical Practices for the Choral Writer
8. Modern Musical Techniques
9. Non-traditional Notation

We cannot afford to be content with the mimeographed repertoire list of yesterday. Increased exposure of singers and students through mass communications media has changed and enlarged their musical experience, and we all need to be sensitive to such change. The teacher who is indifferent, or who denounces a new musical experience as too commercial, or as an unacceptable compromise, has already taken a step away from those experiences many singers hold to be important. The more aware conductors among us will benefit from including various types of music in the experience of their singers.

There are times when we will find it advantageous to entertain as well as to educate an audience, but there are also times when music should be introduced for its educational value alone. In a sense, any music a person particularly enjoys is entertainment to that person, and the music may also have valid educational worth. The choral music of William Billings and Charles Ives, for example, has not long been considered to be concert music that will be accepted enthusiastically by performers and audiences alike. However, this music has been performed to much acclaim during recent years, just as the more standard repertoire of the European "masters" has long been accepted and performed by choruses in this country. You can profit from programming established repertoire, but there are times when you may want to go beyond usual, established musical limits.

After the music has been selected, the next step is to prepare the musical score for rehearsal and performance. Your ability to analyze and to prepare the score will determine to a large extent how effective you will be in rehearsal. Professional conductors place a premium on saving rehearsal time because every extra minute spent costs additional money. While we should not expect young students to possess the voices or experience of professional singers, there are techniques of preparation and organization that will benefit conductors of choral music at any level.

Although teachers and conductors regularly perform choral music from the Renaissance to the present day, there is a need to clarify performance practices. A conductor may have a preference for, or feel most comfortable in, performing music of one particular period in the history of western music, but few choirs can successfully limit performance to such specialized repertoire. While it is not to be advocated that we become "all things to all people," the time is here when we all need to be conversant with the major forms and styles currently in use.

Of course, our training has considerable influence on our ability to work with choruses. It would be helpful if colleges and universities would give more time to training their choral students specifically in score preparation. Every music teacher has taken classes in general music theory, but such subjects as score preparation still are not covered sufficiently at most colleges and universities. Also, there are courses in choral conducting which give practical experience in that aspect of the art. But, again, the training often does not include real instruction in the preparation of music for rehearsal and performance. Part II of this book is included with the intention of helping to fill this gap.

The text is often given a secondary position in relation to the music. Some choral conductors appear to believe the text needs little or no special treatment. Of course, the text is an integral part of the choral score, and the successful conductor will recognize its value. It is important to associate the musical text with the voice, and there are techniques of associating the text with musical rhythm. While the subject most properly should be included in a book on voice training, a portion of Part II is devoted to discussing topics relevant to understanding the relationship of music and text.

While the text is important, the music itself is no less significant. As the notes are mastered and as matters of intonation are corrected, we must also give careful attention to such elements as melody, harmony, and rhythm.

Each of us can refine our score preparation, and we should periodically examine the techniques we use. We may teach in a program where music of only modest difficulty can be used, or we may conduct a choir capable of performing the most difficult music available. In either of these situations, careful and special attention to score preparation will aid the choir in performing at its maximum capability. The development of a carefully constructed method of working with the choral score will enable us and our singers to be more efficient in the use of rehearsal time; also, the final result will be more musical.

Part III is devoted to the writing of music; the arranging, editing, and composing of music may be a necessary part of building a fine choral program. Frequently, it is this area which gives choral conductors the most difficulty. While it is recognized that some teachers will have more aptitude for arranging and writing than do their colleagues, Part III includes ideas and techniques of writing which will be helpful to all choral conductors.

Although there is a vast quantity of choral music available today, there are times when available editions and arrangements do not fulfill the unique requirements of a particular choral group. Perhaps the need for us to make musical changes and additions is greatest when we are working with young singers, or when we are teaching in a modest choral program. But a large number of us are involved in, or know others who are involved in, choral situations which require more than the usual music selection and preparation. You will be of more benefit to your choral program if the ideas and techniques discussed in Part III are absorbed and applied.

The active choral conductor has readily available a group of singers who can sing his arrangements, and such a point should not be minimized. Your own singers will tend to give a sympathetic reading to your manuscript. While you should not use large segments of rehearsal time in this kind of endeavor, it is quite possible for you to put your own music before your choir to the mutual benefit of you and your singers.

Part III will include brief discussions of the work of the editor, the arranger, and the composer. There is no doubt that some conductors are more fluent at composing or arranging, but this is no different from saying that some teachers sing better than others. While, ideally, every choral conductor should be a performer, in actual practice such is not the case; a parallel situation exists in the area of writing music. If you have received training as a choral conductor and if you will apply the principles and techniques presented, the result will be to improve your music writing. There are many books and articles concerning orchestration and arranging for band, but relatively little is written about the subject in the field of choral music.

There is non-traditional notation which is important to those who work in the choral field today, and many examples of new notation are included.

Working with the three areas discussed in this book is essential if we choral conductors are to realize the full potential of our singers. It is with this point in mind that you are urged to consider the specific points discussed. And this study is dedicated to working with people through choral music in order to attain the highest level of musical achievement possible. Special mention is due the University of Missouri-St. Louis for providing a sabbatical leave which greatly facilitated the preparation of the manuscript.

Kenneth E. Miller

Contents

PART ONE

CHORAL MUSIC SELECTION

1

Sources and Guidelines
for Selecting Choir Music

In this chapter, you will find answers to such important matters as where to look for new music, how to use rental and lending libraries, and the use of criteria in selecting music for your choir. If you follow the recommendations discussed here, you will consistently build a quality library of choral music as economically as is possible.

THE NEED TO KNOW YOUR SINGERS

Selecting music is a specific task which each conductor undertakes for himself. Choosing music for performance should not be delegated to another person, and it should not be undertaken without full knowledge of the singers and actual circumstances of the performance for which the music is being selected. Those of us who have had the responsibility of selecting music for choirs, have learned first hand of the difficulties involved. Most of us choose "safe" programs when we must select music without first knowing the singers. But such selection of music is not sufficient to challenge our performers over a period of several months or years.

The need to know the actual singers is particularly important when we are working with young choir members. If we are auditioning from an inexhaustible supply of experienced talent, we may first choose the music and then select singers specifically to perform the music chosen. But to know the singers before selecting music is preferred in almost every circumstance. Then we can choose music that will be interesting and well

17

received by those who will spend hours of rehearsal time working toward its proper performance.

Every choral program has strong years and lean years. This year you may have mature singers in every section. But next year several of those experienced and solid choir members may have graduated, and one or more sections may not be able to handle music on the level sung previously. For example, one year the tenor section may be mature but another year it may be necessary to use low altos to supplement the tenors, or some singers in the alto section may actually have low soprano voices. We can adapt this discussion to any number of varied circumstances, but the conclusion in each instance will be that you need to know your singers before the music is chosen.

THE ROLE OF THE CONDUCTOR

Selecting music is one of the most important tasks we choral conductors undertake. To choose music for a choir is to make basic decisions about the direction of the year's rehearsals and concerts. We not only need to know our singers, but we should take into consideration our own musical strengths and weaknesses. No musician feels equally qualified in all styles and musical periods, and it is important for each of us to take into account our own musical taste without discounting the tastes of our choir members.

Our own background and musical taste is reflected in the music we choose, and it is important that we always work to broaden our musical base. Programs chosen by a conductor will give much information about the musical background, taste and capability of that person, just as those same programs will tell something about the choir's capability. Select high school and college/university choirs can perform almost any music if the music is well taught. But not every piece of music selected will reach the performance level desired, and there are times when plans must be altered. We should be ready to make changes in planned concert programs so as to reflect the best performance by our choir at any particular time.

Careful attention should be given to the difficulty of music chosen. The preferred plan is to include one or two compositions that fully test the musical capacity of the choir, and this difficult music will best be programmed with other less demanding repertoire. We will want to include music in each category—easy, medium, difficult—on most, if not all, concert programs, with much of the music chosen being classified as medium in difficulty for that particular choir.

The choral music teacher in a school has much more opportunity to design a curriculum to meet the particular needs of the students than do individual teachers in most other areas. Teachers in such subject areas as history, English, science and mathematics normally follow an adopted curriculum, and they are expected to cover the curriculum in a specified number of class periods. We choral teachers have much more freedom in planning a year's teaching; also, we assume the time consuming responsibility of making different plans each year. While the selection of new music each year takes much time, this primary step in planning always must be given serious attention.

WHERE TO LOOK FOR MUSIC

The first step in selecting music is to know what is available and where to find the music desired. There are many sources, and every teacher should become familiar with standard sources of music.

Some of the best ways of finding new repertoire are to attend concerts and to collect printed programs of concerts given by other choirs. Many conductors exchange program tips, and informal conversations can produce some of the most productive ideas. While we may not always agree on the merits of the music selected, it is quite helpful to engage other teachers and conductors in conversation and to have the benefit of their ideas. Every one of us not only needs to have others confirm the validity of music we select, but there are times when it may be helpful for us to have the benefit of contrary opinions.

Reading sessions, clinics and workshops that give the participants the opportunity to sight-read many new publications, are offered in most areas of the country and are good sources for choosing new music. Such sessions allow participants to become acquainted with much music firsthand.

Music companies, colleges and universities frequently offer reading sessions, clinics and workshops during the summer months, often at a very nominal charge. Normally lasting from one day to a week, these sessions acquaint teachers with a greater variety of music than the average person will learn anywhere else during the year. Also, these sessions offer us an excellent opportunity to exchange ideas with fellow musicians.

Choral conventions offer an opportunity to hear auditioned choirs perform the music of their choice, and conventions also offer the best opportunity to visually examine large quantities of music. New music of most publishing houses can be examined at the publishers' booths, and composers and arrangers may be available to discuss their own compositions. Conventions of the American Choral Directors Association are recommended, in particular, for learning new music, but more general meetings of such organizations as the Music Educators National Conference can also be valuable.

Professional magazines, journals and publishers' mailing lists aid in keeping us informed of new publications. We should be included on publishers' mailing lists, and there are times when it will be best for us to take advantage of publishers' "on approval" service. We can examine the music at our leisure if we ask for complimentary copies, and we should keep publishers notified of our current mailing address.

While the above sources of music are valuable primarily for learning new publications, there are books and catalogues which serve as more permanent sources for learning repertoire. While we will always want to search for new publications, we will be well advised to keep in mind that a significant portion of the music programmed each year should be selected from the excellent tested and established choral literature. The publications listed below contain a wealth of valuable information:

> *An Annotated Inventory of Distinctive Choral Literature for Performance at the High School Level.* Ed. Margaret B. Hawkins. American Choral Directors Association, 1976.
>
> *Catalogue of Published American Choral Music.* New York: National Federation of Music Clubs, 1955.
>
> *Choral Music in Print*, two volumes. Philadelphia: Musicdata, Inc., 1974; supplement, 1976.
>
> *Handbuch der Chormusik*, two volumes. ed. Erich Valentin. Regenburg: Gustav Bosse, 1958.
>
> *Selected List of Choruses for Women's Voices*, third edition. Compiled by Arthur Ware Locke and Charles K. Fassett. Northampton: Smith College, 1964.
>
> *Selected List of Music for Men's Voices.* Ed. J. Merrill Knapp. Princeton: Princeton University Press, 1952.

How to Make Good Use of Rental and Lending Libraries

Every school music department and every choral group needs to build a permanent music library, but the use of a rental or lending library can aid in stretching the budget. If the lack of a sufficient budget is a factor in limiting the music you program, then you will profit from investigating one of the following rental or lending libraries.

No one should be asked to work with a budget so limited that the choral program must rely on a rental or lending library for a major portion of the music used during any one year. Also, some music is available only by renting directly from the publisher. The rental and lending libraries listed below are not associated with any publishers; they are independent organizations and they will make quantities of music available to choirs at a very nominal charge. You will need to contact the library of interest to you, in order to receive specific information about current financial arrangements.

Rental and lending libraries for choral music include the following:

> Drinker Choral Library
> The Free Library of Philadelphia
> Logan Square
> Philadelphia, PA 19103
>
> Mapleson
> 208 North Broadway
> Lindenhurst, L.I., N.Y. 11757
>
> New York Choral Society
> 165 West 57th Street
> New York, N.Y. 10018
>
> The Collegiate Chorale, Inc.
> 130 West 56th Street
> New York, N.Y. 10019

CRITERIA IN SELECTING CHORAL MUSIC

It should now be clear to all of us that one of the most important steps in preparing a choral program is to choose the actual music to be sung. Many of us have seen conductors make unwise choices because they had no definite criteria to use in judging the music being considered; they simply "liked" a piece of music or "thought" it would be "good" for their choir. Selecting repertoire under such circumstances rarely produces the best results. It is necessary for us to use criteria in selecting music if we are to be successful in building a significant and balanced library of choral music.

Music Selection Checklist

The following eighteen points are listed as criteria to be followed, but they are not intended to be listed in any order of importance. If you check these eighteen points before selecting a composition, you will choose your music carefully.

1. Choose music which is appealing to you.
2. Judge the educational worth of the text.
3. Choose music with a compatible text.
4. Attention should be given to the validity of the edition.
5. The music you choose should have a text which is easily sung.

6. Range and tessitura are significant considerations.

7. The composition needs to be rhythmically, harmonically and melodically interesting

8. The voice parts should be easily sung.

9. The best performance will be achieved if the music appeals to the singers and audience.

10. The singers will be most comfortable if the music enhances the strong points of the choir.

11. The music should help to build a balanced choral library.

12. If an arrangement, the composition will be best if it reflects the spirit of the original.

13. Choose music which will be a wise financial investment.

14. Determine if the music is within the performing capability of your choir.

15. There needs to be time to learn the music.

16. The music should contribute to your educational goals.

17. Check to see that required instruments are available.

18. It is important that the instrumental accompaniment be musically integrated with the choral composition.

There may be times when we will need music for a specific purpose, and on such an occasion one or more of the criteria may be omitted. But when we are looking for music to perform in concert, and when we are looking for music to enhance the value of our educational program, then we will profit from limiting the selection of music to those compositions which fulfill the criteria listed above. The remainder of the chapter will be devoted to a further explanation of the eighteen criteria.

1. Choose Music Which Is Appealing to You

This may be one of the most basic criteria. It is necessary for you to be interested in the music performed, for only then will you give the music your best attention. You and I have experienced choral music in many and varied circumstances, and we have developed a taste for a certain type of music. While every one of us must take into account the interests of our singers and the audience, we should also satisfy our own taste.

You have had the experience of choosing music because it was of interest to someone else, and then you also may have had the experience of wishing you had not chosen that composition. Perhaps the composition did not really appeal to you, and you as the conductor could not give the music your full and enthusiastic support. The result was that you did not really rehearse the music in sufficient depth to achieve the fullest performance potential from your choir.

The music you choose is most often a reflection of your own interest and background. It is not difficult to look at choral programs and find out a great deal about the conductor as a teacher and musician. (I am not suggesting that revealing the conductor's musical self is bad or that we should try to cover up our true musical identity.)

2. Judge the Educational Worth of the Text

In this discussion, we are not referring to questions such as "Did Bach use carefully chosen texts?" We are referring to the fact that some music heard on radio, television, and in concert includes texts which are not suitable teaching material in an educational situation. If you teach in a high school, the music will be most suitable if the text set can easily be understood by the students who will do the singing. Of course, the same is true for any situation. But I have seen conductors impose music on choirs who would never be able to give a real interpretation of the work because the singers were not capable of understanding what was being expressed in the text.

We have many classes and workshops that deal with the need to study and perfect the music; now you are being asked to give equal consideration to the text.

3. Choose Music with a Compatible Text

Not only should the text be worth singing, it should also be carefully set to music. Since choral music does include a text of some kind, and since both text and music have natural accents, it is necessary to consider such matters as meter in both music and text. Does the meter of the text and music coincide, or is there rhythmic conflict?

Perhaps the highest praise we can give to a setting of a text is to observe that it seems to have been meant for that particular music. Of course, it was the composer who chose the text, and it was the composer who took care to see that the natural rhythmic flow of the text was not destroyed by the music.

It is appropriate to say a few words about translations, for they can be a source of special problems. While there is no hard and fast rule concerning translations, there are often difficulties inherent in changing a text from one language to another. As most choral conductors know, the metrical composition of a translation may be so different from the original that musical stresses fall on unimportant words or syllables, and all manner of

vocal problems appear. Unless a translation enhances the music and unless
it is more easily understood by the singers and audience than the original,
you should think long and hard before choosing to perform a text in translation. If the choice is to sing a bad translation or not sing the composition at
all, most often it is better to choose other music to perform.

The text provides subject matter and rhythmic underlay for the music.
Music well set capitalizes on those qualities in the text and carries the
emotional and imaginative content of the text to a height which the text
alone can not attain. When this happens, we find an advantageous association of text and music, and fine singing can result.

4. Attention Should Be Given to the Validity of the Edition

While there are many good editions of music available, there are also
editions which should not be used. To evaluate the field of editing is to
undertake a large subject that we cannot properly cover here. Therefore,
the discussion at this time will be limited to a few of the most important
points.

Editors who also have been successful choral conductors have been
known to publish editions of music with markings that show only their
interpretation of the composition. While there is no doubt that every
choral conductor has the right to interpret the music he conducts, there is
also no doubt that an edition of the music itself should contain only the
composer's music plus any editorial markings clearly marked as such. Then
and only then can we know what the composer really wrote.

Editions exist that contain dynamic marks in music which was actually
composed before dynamics existed as a known musical element. Also,
editions exist today which show measure bars and meter signatures when
the original had no measure bars or metrical indications. Here again, the
editor who added these markings often has not shown them to have been
his own work, and the unsuspecting choral conductor may simply take the
markings to be the indication of the composer rather than the editor.

Editions of choral music exist that have almost completely changed
the original text, that have changed most or all of an entire voice part, and
that have added an accompaniment when the original music actually had
none. Any such treatment of a choral composition is in clear violation of the
best interests of both the composer and the performer.

This brief discussion, then, includes a plea that we study choral performance practices as they relate to the history of music. The next step is to
purchase only those scores which clearly follow the careful practice of
preserving what the composer actually wrote. All editorial markings are to
be clearly labelled as such, and more will be said about this subject in
Chapter 6.

5. *The Music You Choose Should Have a Text Which Is Easily Sung*

It is possible for the text of a choral composition to fulfill other criteria and yet not be the best selection for your choir. There are texts that simply cannot be easily sung, and, unless you work with very capable singers, you will be well advised to take care to select texts which do not present peculiar difficulties.

Twentieth century choral music in all probability presents more potential textual problems than do compositions of previous musical periods. This is particularly true of avant-garde compositions, but there are also many other compositions which require the singers to master sounds other than those found in traditional texts.

If you agree that the text is an important part of a choral composition and that the text needs to be understood by the singers and audience alike, then the necessity for supplying singers with compositions that have meaningful texts and that offer no unusual vocal problems appears to be self-evident. An examination of settings of the same text by two or more composers will make increasingly clear the fact that your singers can more easily sing one setting than another. For example, consider the Mass as set by Palestrina, J.S. Bach, Beethoven and Bernstein.

This criterion has two facets: (1) the text may contain actual vocal sounds which are unusually difficult to sing, and (2) the relationship of a text to the music of a particular composer may add unnecessary problems.

6. *Range and Tessitura Are Significant Considerations*

Range and tessitura are important considerations when we select music. Trained singers know their own range limitations and they can help to make such determinations for themselves, but it is the conductor who makes these decisions for his choir. Every choir will sound best when the notes of the compositions being performed fall comfortably within the singing ranges of the singers.

Voices do not always fall neatly into exact ranges, but most untrained voices will remain within the following limits.

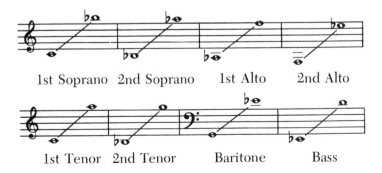

1st Soprano 2nd Soprano   1st Alto   2nd Alto

1st Tenor 2nd Tenor   Baritone   Bass

- If the voice ranges do exceed the limits shown above, it is quite important for you to examine the music with great care.
- You should observe how often the usual ranges are exceeded, and it is important to look at the vowel sounds required on those extreme notes.

Here we return to the first topic discussed in this chapter—the need to know your singers. If you know the voices you are to use, you can then determine if the musical range is within the vocal limits of those singers.

Tessitura is usually described as the average pitch position of a composition. Music which has many high pitches may be said to have a "high" tessitura, and a composition having many low notes is said to have a "low" tessitura. Extremely high or low notes may be the cause of real vocal discomfort, but a tessitura generally out of the range of the singers also can be the cause of vocal strain. Any of these situations will increase the possibility of compromising the sound of your choir.

When extreme pitches or tessitura occur in any one voice part it is necessary to observe (1) the dynamic marking, (2) if that part is supported by the other voices or if it is exposed, and (3) if all the voices are in an unusual range at the same time.

7. The Composition Needs to Be Rhythmically, Harmonically, and Melodically Interesting

These are the three musical elements that most influence the selection of choral music; if these elements are sufficiently strong, then the music will almost certainly have sufficient intrinsic value to be interesting through rehearsal and performance. These elements have a definite relationship, but they can best be discussed individually.

1. Rhythm is the most basic element in music, and choirs generally have more problems rhythmically than harmonically or melodically. My observation at choral reading sessions has been that many conductors could profit from more intensive attention to the correct performance of musical rhythm.

Rhythm often shifts within a composition, and this may cause problems. First, you should determine if the composer has chosen a common pulse, even though the meter has changed. For example, the rhythmic value of a quarter note may equal the rhythmic value of an eighth note in a different meter. Another type of change is seen, for example, in Morley's madrigal, "My Bonny Lass She Smileth," where there is a change from duple to triple meter, and singers and conductor alike must take unusual care if this change is to be negotiated smoothly.

In rehearsing difficult rhythmic passages, scanning is recommended.

To scan is to isolate musical and textual rhythm and repeat those elements together on a medium to medium-high spoken pitch. Scanning has the advantage of eliminating all matters other than those which relate to musical and textual rhythm, and this technique will clear up rhythmic problems much more quickly than if we try to include the rehearsal of harmony and melody at the same time.

You can scan a new composition at first reading and in this way determine very quickly the level of rhythmic difficulty of a composition.

2. The harmony of a composition will fall into traditional or twentieth century patterns, and choral conductors often will find more problems in recent music. Harmonic progressions in any composition are basic to determining the flow of the music. If the progressions are natural and logical, the music will move in the same manner. If the progressions are awkward or forced, the music will seem contrived and unnatural.

It is important for the conductor to determine the basic harmonic language on first examination of the score, and the following are some of the questions you should ask yourself.

- Is the music tonal?
- Is the writing consistent, or are there strong and weak progressions?
- Does the harmonic structure enhance the text?

3. The importance of the melody may be more obvious than matters concerning rhythm and harmony. Almost everyone enjoys music which has a melody they can remember. But not all melody will be as obvious as it is in an art song, for example. Sometimes it is necessary to examine music over a period of time before the true melodic content becomes clear.

Melody forms the dominant musical line of a composition, but the melody may not always be found in the obvious voice part. One technique that may be useful is to underline the major melodic content before beginning to rehearse the music. In this way, the score clearly identifies the melody, and rehearsal time may be saved because of the resulting clear and instant melodic identification.

8. *The Voice Parts Should Be Easily Sung*

This topic relates to the presence or absence of a vocal line. All rules of musical composition may be followed, but still the music may not be easily sung. Music which is not easily sung is sometimes called "instrumental." By the use of such a term, we usually mean to say that the intervals of one or more voice parts do not aid the singer in developing a concept of the vocal line; the music can be easily played, but the part is not easily sung. It will be more difficult for choral directors who have had little actual voice training to successfully analyze and teach the concept of vocal line.

Experienced and trained singers will work toward the objective of creating a singable vocal line in any music they perform. But young choir members need more coaching before they can develop such understanding. Only with maturity of understanding in singing the vocal line will the choral sound of your singers approach the maximum potential of the choir. Maturity in understanding the physical requirements of singing and maturity in understanding the music are both important, but too often the lack of specific stress on matters related to the singing of the vocal line in a composition prohibits musical performance from reaching the optimal level possible.

While you may be able to make some determination about vocal line just by looking at the music, you will not actually understand this aspect of the score until you sing the music yourself. Take time to sing every composition and every voice part in your own range before passing out the music for rehearsal.

9. The Best Performance Will Be Achieved if the Music Appeals to the Singers and Audience

You will be most successful in your teaching if much of the music you choose for performance appeals to the singers and to the audience. It has often been demonstrated that when singers enjoy the music they perform, they sing at their best and their enthusiasm is transmitted to the audience.

This is not to suggest that you should limit your entire choice of music to the musical, cultural, psychological and academic levels your singers exhibit at the beginning of the school year. To place such limitations on your choral program will reduce or eliminate too much of its educational value. We should include some music in our choral rehearsal sessions which stretches the musical and educational horizons of our performers; perhaps we also will want to include music in public concerts which will broaden the horizons of the audience. But we must be cautious in programming music that is on a different level artistically from the music generally understood by our audience. For example, I can think of conductors who lost their positions because they programmed too much avant-garde music and the audience began to stay away from concerts.

Taking into account the musical and cultural tastes of our singers and audiences is not a simple matter. Each of us must first satisfy ourselves about how adventurous a piece of music to put on a concert program. But we will be most successful if we also take into consideration the musical interests and needs of those students in the choral program and those who come to hear the concerts. Social circumstances as well as actual musical techniques should be taken into consideration.

10. The Singers Will Be Most Comfortable if the Music Enhances the Strong Points of the Choir

It is possible that you will find a composition you want your choir to perform, and that music will fulfill all criteria with the exception of this one. Strengths of choirs do change from year to year, and you should not, of course, program music which will accentuate the weaknesses of your choir.

No recitalist chooses repertoire which "isn't right" for him, and the conductor should take as much care in choosing music for his choir to perform. Sometimes it will be possible to identify exactly the musical problem that makes it difficult to program a particular composition—i.e., the sopranos may not be able to sustain the required high notes, or the choir may not have the capability of performing a particularly intricate rhythmic pattern. But there are times when you will not be able to identify exactly why you do not feel a composition is "right" for your particular choir. Intuitive judgment must be a factor, but there are times when we should be willing to rehearse such music and give the choir an opportunity to grow into performing music which we had originally doubted they would be able to perform. However, if the music does not begin to sound right after a few rehearsals, it should be retained for performance at a later time.

11. The Music Should Help to Build a Balanced Choral Library

If you have all the funds you need to buy multiple copies of any music you can use, you are fortunate indeed. Most of us work within a budget, and it is important that we use the budget efficiently. A balanced choral library contains much music which will not quickly become obsolete.

Compositions discussed in Chapter 2 will include music from the various musical periods and styles, and the choices will serve as representative examples of recommended compositions. But it is necessary for you to know your choral library and build around your present collection. If you have been in your present position several years, the choral library reflects your own ideas and taste. If you move into a new position, it is only natural that you will want to use your own music. But you should also become acquainted with the existing choral library. Within a three-or four-year cycle, a choir in any school should sing compositions from the Renaissance to the Twentieth Century. While there may be some difference in the list of specific compositions which will best suit your particular situation, composers such as Palestrina, Handel, Bach, Mozart, and Brahms have produced choral music which has stood for centuries. You may believe that recent music should make up a considerable portion of the music you perform, but you cannot afford to overlook the rich musical legacy which we have inherited from previous times.

12. If An Arrangement, the Composition Will Be Best If It Reflects the Spirit of the Original

We shall not at this time go into the matter of deciding if arrangements should be used; the present discussion will assume that you do use choral arrangements at some time. My purpose here is to give some direction to you in the use of arrangements. Perhaps this discussion is more appropriate to folk songs and spirituals than to other more complex music, but there are art compositions that have been arranged for chorus and that still possess their original charm.

There has been a tendency of some to overarrange, and it should be understood that, as a rule, one should not change the original melodic portion of a composition. Occasionally there may be a folk melody that can be strengthened by some slight alteration, but no one should enter into such a practice without exercising great care.

Folk songs and spirituals are among the less complex classifications of choral music, and the wise arranger will not feel it necessary to add so much that the original simplicity is obscured. On the other hand, it would be equally indiscreet to take the choral theme from Beethoven's Ninth Symphony, for example, and arrange it in the style of a simple, unobtrusive composition.

An example of an art song which has been set quite successfully as choral music is "Sure On This Shining Night" by Samuel Barber. While the original composition is for solo voice, the composition has been set for four-part chorus; the original charm has been preserved, and the arrangement adds a fine composition to the choral repertoire.

13. Choose Music Which Will Be a Wise Financial Investment

Most of us work within a budget, and the price of music has increased sharply in recent years. Inflation is a factor in influencing our decision to buy, rent or borrow choral music, and the situation will not quickly be changed. Therefore, budget considerations are basic to making additions to the choral library.

There are ways of stretching a tight budget, and some of the following considerations will help to make the budget go farther. Octavo music may be more expensive than purchasing the same compositions in a collection. It will be wise to check such collections as *Five Centuries of Choral Music* and to compare the cost of that collection with the cost of buying octavo copies. Often several compositions in a collection will be usable over a period of time, and you can make quite a saving in making such a purchase.

If you teach in a school system of some size, you may be able to borrow copies of a desired composition from another school, or you may be able to use a central library.

Choosing where to purchase music can make a difference in cost; music houses differ in the amount of discount they will give choral accounts. You may be able to save a significant portion of your budget just by shopping around for a supplier where you can get good service and a larger quantity discount.

14. Determine If the Music Is Within the Performing Capability of Your Choir.

While this point may touch upon criteria discussed previously, particularly numbers six and ten, this discussion is as different from those matters as is the difference between musical rhythm and meter. Specific consideration of such matters as range and tessitura must not be overlooked, but this discussion views the selection of music for your choir in a more comprehensive way. Range and tessitura may be within the grasp of your singers, but the composition still may not be within the actual performing capability of your music.

A further question appropriate to this point is: Can the meaning of the music be comprehended so that an emotionally mature performance can result? Emotion is a proper element of music. We all have witnessed performances which went to extreme in either "playing up" the emotional element excessively or in using the technique of singing correctly but with no emotional communication. Obviously, neither extreme is desirable. But it is important for your singers to be able to communicate the real content of the music both emotionally and intellectually. When this is done and when the technical matters have been performed correctly, a mature musical performance results. To leave out or to minimize any of these elements · will inevitably result in a less than optimal performance, and your choir will have performed at a level lower than its true capability.

You must make a judgment when you select the music as to whether your choir will be capable of handling not only the technical matters but also the emotional and intellectual elements necessary for real communication through choral singing.

15. There Needs to Be Time to Learn the Music

There are choral conductors who have been well trained in teaching the elements of music but who have little sense of schedule or timing. This criterion deals with a very practical matter; along with all other criteria, there must be adequate rehearsal time to work on perfecting the music.

One of the most frustrating experiences for your singers is to spend many hours of rehearsal time on music that they enjoy and then come to the realization, just a few days before the concert, that the composition is not ready to be performed. You delete the music from the program, and, while some benefit may have been derived from general acquaintance with the composition, you and your singers all feel a sense of defeat. Planning rehearsal time wisely will prevent such an unnecessary waste of time, but nothing can replace the need for basic musicianship.

16. The Music Should Contribute to Your Educational Goals

Every choral program will be most valuable to the singers if educational goals are defined and made known to all who participate in the program. While there may be a place for show music and music for recreation, there can be little justification for awarding academic credit to your singers unless you provide music equivalent in educational value to subject matter presented in other credit courses within your school. Having defined the goals, your choice of music should be consistent with those goals.

Valid educational goals for the choral program may include the following:

1. Acquaint the singers with representative compositions of each musical period, Renaissance to the Twentieth Century, within a cycle of three or four years.

2. Increasingly challenge the singers to perform music which is technically, emotionally and/or intellectually on a more mature level as they progress through the choral program.

3. Acquaint the more advanced singers with nontraditional notation as well as standard notational practices.

4. Briefly present general musical and cultural background information that will give your singers a more complete understanding of the compositions that they sing.

17. Check to See That Required Instruments Are Available

Unaccompanied choral music should be sung regularly, but no choir should limit its repertoire to unaccompanied compositions or to the use of piano accompaniment. There is an important repertoire which uses one or more non-keyboard instruments, and this criterion deals with those compositions. This discussion will not be concerned with the ability of choral conductors to conduct music using instruments; every one of us should be capable of handling instruments in a choral situation.

It is generally known that common practice in the Renaissance and earlier times involved the support of voices by instruments and/or the substitution of instruments for voice parts in most music. Often those instruments were not specifically designated, and this point gives us considerable latitude in determining the best instrument(s) to use in a particular performance.

Baroque choral music used instrumental support in the bass line, if not a complete instrumental ensemble. The Baroque era is the time of the continuo. Even when an instrumental ensemble is indicated, you may substitute if you do not have an instrument called for but do have an instrument with similar tonal characteristics. For example, currently published editions of *Messiah* clearly show that Handel himself used different vocal solo voice classifications and different instruments in the ensemble for different performances. While we have a traditional idea of how *Messiah* should be performed, if Handel varied his performing forces we can do the same.

Music composed after the Baroque era more specifically identifies definite instrumentation, and there is little valid reason to substitute in this choral music. If it is a choice of performing with keyboard accompaniment or not giving your singers experience in singing major choral compositions, then you should use the piano or organ. But you should make it clear to everyone that you are not performing the composition as originally written because of limited instrumental resources.

The use of instruments is an important consideration, and their proper use can add much to a choral concert. But the absence of an occasional instrument specified in the score should not be used as a reason to deprive your singers and audiences of the experience of becoming acquainted with the monuments of choral music.

18. It Is Important That the Instrumental Accompaniment Be Musically Integrated with the Choral Composition

We, as choral conductors, give much attention to the singing of our choirs, but we sometimes do not give equal attention to the accompaniment. We should be concerned with two points: (1) did the composer supply the composition with an integrated accompaniment, and (2) is the accompanist we have selected capable of integrating the accompaniment with the composition as a whole?

A "practiced eye" can quickly determine if the composer has kept the accompaniment musically integrated, or if the accompaniment has been given so much prominence that it becomes the major musical interest. The pianist who serves as an accompanist does not assume the same role as does a solo pianist, or a pianist performing in a chamber ensemble. An accompanist must know how to make his part balance properly with the chorus, and this is a point which cannot be entirely supplied by the conductor. The accompanist needs to be musically sensitive.

The choice of an accompanist is one of the most important decisions you will make. If a technically capable and musically sensitive student accompanist is available, then you will be giving such a talented person an important musical experience by using him as your accompanist. But you should not allow the progress of the singers to be slowed because of your selection of a less capable accompanist. This may mean that you will use another faculty or staff member to serve in this capacity. There may be a capable accompanist in your community who will donate time or serve in this capacity for a small charge, and such a solid musical accompanist can be a very great help. We would not be overstating the situation if we said that a capable accompanist is the most important member of the choir.

2

Selecting Music for Performance: 45 Recommended Compositions

The following pages contain selected music for mixed choir, female choir, male choir, and chamber choir. This chapter includes a list of forty-five choral compositions which are specially recommended for public performance. Every attempt has been made to see that the list of recommended music includes compositions at all levels of difficulty. Octavo and some medium length works are listed, but my selection does not include oratorios, passions or similar large works. Neither does the list include music specifically chosen for changing voices.

You will find familiar and unfamiliar compositions discussed, but particular attention has been given to including examples which have stood the test of time. The music chosen fulfills criteria listed in Chapter 1, and many compositions have already given hours of pleasure and enjoyment to performers. This kind of pleasure is found only by those who have labored over music sufficiently so that they may ultimately experience the joy of real musical growth.

Since it is clear that we make major decisions about the direction of the choral program when we select the music to be performed by our choirs, the actual music chosen is of basic importance. The annotations included for each of the following compositions are intended to be helpful in selecting music suitable for our choirs.

Compositions for mixed voices are more numerous than are compositions for men or women. This selection simply reflects the fact that there are more performances by mixed choirs. Yet, significant examples of choral music appropriate to all usual voice combinations have been included.

Many more matters to consider in program building for public performance will be included in Chapter 4. In this chapter, the discussion is pointed directly to those musical matters which are of more particular concern to the composer and to the choral conductor.

To understand the essence of every composition we perform is to have a grasp of those elements of music which are central to communicating with our singers and audiences. Under such circumstances we will be convinced of the worth of the music we have chosen, and the music we perform can come alive at the actual moment of performance. Such a point of view does not advocate "playing down" to audiences. It is important that our singers, including those who are enrolled in courses in schools, be challenged at some time to achieve their maximum growth and such growth includes actual performance.

My comments about each composition are not intended to substitute for musical analysis. Rather, the comments give a brief introduction to the composition; they include unusual musical difficulties, if any, and they describe the general character of the composition. It is recommended that every conductor start with these comments and follow up with matters that ultimately must be considered when preparing for any specific performance.

MUSIC FOR THE MIXED CHOIR

Since more choral concerts are presented by mixed choirs than by men or women alone, the category is divided into two separate lists: (1) the young choir, and (2) the advanced choir.

The Young Choir

Barber, Samuel   **Sure on this Shining Night**

Barber himself set this original art song for chorus, and the choral setting can be sung equally well. This is a lovely melody and the music contains no particular technical problems. But it will be necessary to have a tenor section which can sustain an independent melody as well as balance the other sections of the chorus.

This is music which can be programmed as a contrasting piece on a concert program, or it may be used for such a special occasion as graduation. The most mature requirement of this music is for the singers to be able to sustain a legato sound while they also successfully negotiate the subtle dynamic changes.

SATB   G. Schirmer 10864

Berger, Jean   **A Rose Touched by the Sun's Warm Rays**

This is a simple melody with voice ranges quite within the capability of a young choir. Reminiscent of the melodies of some early Romantic composers of lieder, this composition has some independence of parts. But there is nothing that will give any choir unusual problems. Of great importance in this simple music will be the ability of the singers to sustain a vocal line through the careful coordination of breath, diction, and musical rhythm. The composition will make good music for teaching and interesting music for performance.

SATB   Augsburg 11-0953

Colgrass, Michael   **Beautiful People**

Colgrass created a relatively easy composition for mixed chorus in which the soprano and alto sections often sing in unison to emphasize the melodic line. The piano part adds an extra dimension to the music, and you will want to choose your pianist with care. This music is from *Best Wishes U.S.A.* and has gentle modern character in both the text and music. The subject matter is idealistic and may appeal, in particular, to young singers and others who have a particular interest in people-to-people subject matter.

SATB   Carl Fischer CM8010

Fauré, Gabriel   **Comfort All Ye My People**

We know Fauré best for his Requiem, but this octavo makes a fine addition to the repertoire for mixed chorus. The music is in three general sections, with the first and last sections being for four-part chorus. The second section is for the soprano and tenor sections followed by a duet for the tenor and bass sections. The music is quite melodic, and the rhythmic motion is gentle and steady. The soprano and tenor often sing together at the interval of a third or sixth, and the alto and bass also are frequently paired. This is singable and interesting music which will be of special interest to a young choir.

SATB   Carl Fischer CM8017

Mendelssohn, Felix   **Heilig**

Mendelssohn's music has often been performed, and it is difficult to choose one representative octavo choral composition of his. "Heilig" (Holy, Holy, Holy) was chosen because it is a fine composition, but also because it represents music for double SATB chorus. This music sounds quite big, but it is not difficult.

The music moves primarily in half-note block chords, and those imitative portions that do exist are quite traditional. There is little need for subtle dynamic shading. Any choir capable of dividing into two groups, capable of making both soft and full dynamic levels sound with consistent tone, and capable of negotiating ordinary imitative passages will find this rewarding music to sing.

SATB-SATB   G. Schirmer 12005

Stravinsky, Igor   **Pater Noster**

This music can logically be paired with *Ave Maria* to form a group of two short Stravinsky pieces. Neither presents any real technical difficulties, and this is quite a beautiful setting of the Lord's prayer. If your singers have some experience singing chant they will understand the kind of rhythmic movement necessary to perform this composition well. Composed homophonically, all voice parts move as one, and the movement is determined by the natural rhythm of the text rather than by the varying musical meters. This composition will give the young choir a brief introduction to the music of one of our most revered composers.

SATB   Boosey & Hawkes 1833

Thompson, Randall   **Frostiana**

There is music here for men's chorus and women's chorus, as well as for mixed chorus. This music may be sung individually or as a group. "Choose Something Like a Star" is often sung alone, and, along with *Alleluia*, it represents some of Thompson's most interesting and accessible music.

Frostiana is an outstanding representative of choral music composed for amateur singers. The poetry is by Robert Frost, and the settings are well within the technical and musical limits of almost all secondary school and adult choirs. Compositions such as these deserve to remain in the standard repertoire, along with music of other leading composers.

SATB, TBB, SAA, SSA/TTBB   E.C. Schirmer
1. The Road Not Taken 2. The Pasture 3. Come In 4. The Telephone 5. A Girl's Garden 6. Stopping by Woods on a Snowy Evening 7. Choose Something Like a Star

Vaughan Williams, Ralph   **O Taste and See**

Composed for the coronation ceremony of Queen Elizabeth II in Westminster Abbey, this short motet is for a solo soprano, SATB chorus, and has a brief introduction for organ. The same exquisite melody which serves as the musical basis of this composition is first sung by the soloist and then by the soprano section. The alto, tenor, and bass sections then enter imitatively and ultimately support the melody through firm, traditional chords. This simple and natural composition is not technically difficult, but it does require a mature solo voice to make the music sound.

SATB   Oxford University Press 43P909

Zimmermann, Heinz Werner   **Come, Let Us Praise**

This Christmas carol has no real musical difficulties to overcome in preparing for performance. It is strophic and can be performed in any of the following ways: (1) Unison choir, perhaps with audience participation, with keyboard accompaniment; (2) the choir sings selected stanzas in unison accompaniment and other stanzas in harmony with or without accompaniment; or (3) with a soloist, selected treble or male voices singing some stanzas in unison with the full mixed chorus singing the remaining stanzas. If you conduct a young choir, you will want to consider this music for your Christmas concert.

Unison or SATB   Carl Fischer CM7986

Music for the Advanced Choir

Bach, J.C.   **Ich lasse dich nicht**

This work, "I'll not let Thee go," is for eight-part choir, and it will best be performed in the Baroque tradition which uses organ with a stringed instrument to double the bass line.

The composition is in three distinct sections, and it is, perhaps, J.C. Bach's best-known choral work. In the first part, the first four-part choir makes the statement and the second choir either repeats the statement or answers with new material. In section two, the alto, tenor, and bass sections have short fugue-like statements while the sopranos carry the principle subject matter in the form of an established chorale melody. The same chorale melody, slightly altered, is sung by the sopranos in the third section, which is in the form of a simple strophic hymn-style chorale. In parts two and three, the choirs combine into one SATB chorus. This composition will make a fine addition to the repertoire of an accomplished high school or adult choir.

SATB-SATB   G. Schirmer 8427

Bach, J.S.   **Jesu, meine Freude**

The eleven sections of Bach's third motet include music for large chorus, chamber chorus, and women's voices. Excerpts can be programmed to advantage if you do not wish to program the entire work. In keeping with the Baroque practice of including a continuo, it is best to use an organ or harpsichord, with a stringed instrument to double the bass line.

This is music for the mature singer and musician, and in most instances this should not be the first of Bach's music to be performed by a chorus or conductor. The necessity of sustaining a phrase and/or a mood expressed in the text goes far beyond simply singing correct pitches and rhythmic values. If the conductor of a select high school choir wishes to perform this motet, he should reserve this music for the most mature singers.

SSATB   Peters 6103

Brahms, Johannes   **Weltliche A Cappella Gesänge**

Peters has published ten secular unaccompanied choral compositions from Op. 42 and Op. 62. Most of these compositions are written for SAATBB voice distribution, but they range from SATB to SSAATTBB. There is considerable variety in these ten songs, but the unique melodic content of Brahms' music is ever present. While more difficult than the settings of *Folk Songs* (Marks) and not as well-known as the *Liebeslieder Waltzes* (AMP), this music should receive more attention. If you have a choir of more than average capability, you may want, in particular, to look at "All meine Herzgedanken." There are well-defined meter and key changes, but no particular rhythmic problems. This is music for expanding your repertoire.

SSAATTBB   Peters 3915a

Bruckner, Anton   **Locus Iste**

Bruckner is well-known as a composer of sacred music, and this is one of his finest octavo compositions. While the musical notation is not difficult to master, the proper performance of this music requires that the singers be capable of a mature, sustained vocal sound. This composition has a religious text which loses something in translation. Musically, intensity of choral sound is required at all dynamic levels and vocal ranges to portray the mature dramatic effect required in this composition and in much of

Bruckner's sacred music. If your choir is capable but has not sung any music by Bruckner, you should give this composition careful attention.

SATB   G. Schirmer 12052

Distler, Hugo   **Lo! How a Rose E'er Blooming**

This is a chorale motet from *The Christmas Story*, and the chorale tune is set in six different compositions taken from the larger work. The use of hemiola and other intricate rhythmic patterns in the original chorale tune and in Distler's added parts give this music rhythmic groupings which are more complex than those found in most similar compositions. Most choirs will find proper rhythmic execution to be the most difficult part of this music in the beginning stage of preparation. After the rhythmic figures are properly executed, the phrasing will become clear and the patterns will quite naturally fall into place to give unity to the composition as a whole.

Some or all six settings will make a fine addition to your Christmas concert.

SSAATTBB   Concordia 97-4849

Gombert, Nicolas   **Votre Beauté Plaisante et Lié**

This composition is representative of sixteenth century practice, and it can serve as an educational tool as well as a good addition to concert repertoire. In music of this time, dynamic markings and tempo indications are editorial suggestions, and experienced performers will learn to look past such markings as the interpretation becomes clear.

Because the translation to English, "Your Beauty Binds Me Pleasantly," cannot be effected without making changes in the rhythmic structure of the text, there is an artistic advantage to singing this music in the original language. Musically, it is necessary that every section of the choir be capable of singing an independent vocal line and of making that part fit into the composition as a whole. Some phrases are longer than average, and the careful use of breath support is more important here than in many compositions.

SATB   Belwin-Mills OCT 2327

Grieg, Edvard   **Four Psalms, Op. 74**

These are Grieg's final compositions; the original Norwegian text is by Laurentii (1573-1655); and the English translation is by Percy Grainger. The harmony asks for a rich and full vocal sound, and Grainger writes of this music: "In proving the applicability and effectiveness of post-Wagnerian polyphonic harmonies to and in vocal composition Grieg has given an impetus to choral music that was lacking throughout the major part of the 19th century." The music is based on old Norwegian church melodies. Chorus number two, "God's Son Hath Set Me Free," is for TTBB in B-flat minor while the music for the baritone soloist is in B-flat major. This use of bitonality represents just one instance of interesting, modern, and original writing.

These Pslams are technically challenging, and they require men capable of singing in four parts. But a capable choir will accept the challenge and work toward revealing the real drama inherent in the music and text.

SSAATTBB/baritone solo   Peters 10460

1. How Fair Is Thy Face 2. God's Son Hath Set Me Free 3. Jesus Christ, Our Lord, Is Risen 4. In Heav'n Above

Handel, G.F.   Swell the Full Chorus

The many choruses from Handel's most familiar oratorios are known to almost everyone in music, but *Solomon* is less often performed. "Swell the Full Chorus" is a fine addition to the full-sounding Handel choral literature, and it is a chorus which can be sung with authority by choirs in secondary schools as well as by older singers.

Full instrumentation is available on rental from the publisher, but piano or organ can be used. If a cellist is available, you can add authenticity by having the stringed instrument double the bass line. There is some rather high tessitura in the soprano part, the basses have an interesting melismatic passage in sequence, and the music should not be looked upon as strictly easy. But this is Handel, and the music is almost always chordal and syllabic. Most choirs will find this music very enjoyable to sing.

SATB   Galaxy 1.2144.1

Ives, Charles   Sixty-Seventh Psalm

This composition shows an early example of Ives's use of bitonality—G-minor for the tenors and basses and C-major for the sopranos and altos. While the two keys are unmistakably different, Ives stressed that they were to be thought of as one unified whole. It is probable that this is Ives' most often performed choral composition. Early performances were given by Lehman Engel (1937) and Robert Shaw (1948), and the music is in ABA' form. The first section includes verses one, two and three; the second section includes verses four and five; and the third section includes verses six and seven of the psalm text.

Section A, measures one to fifteen, harmonically is a series of triads, one juxtaposed on the other. In section B, beginning at measure sixteen, there is imitation with alternation between the men and women. The third section, A', begins at measure twenty-seven and, while there is some rhythmic change because of the new text, it generally repeats the substance of the first section. The final chord progression forms a I-IV-I cadence.

A capable choir will accept the musical challenges presented in this music.

SSAATTBB   Associated Music Publishers A-274

Mechem, Kirke   Give Thanks Unto The Lord

If you are looking for unaccompanied music with a full sound and music which will be within the performing capability of most choirs, you will want to look at this score. There are four definite sections, fast-slow-fast-slow, with chordal and some imitative writing. The divisi in the soprano, alto, and bass parts require that a choir have sections which are capable of dividing. But the ranges are not extreme, and clear vocal distinction between those who sing first or second are not required. There are no unusual exposed parts, and most choirs will find this music enjoyable to sing.

SSAATBB   Peters P6213

Puccini, Giacomo   Requiem

The Requiem was composed in Milan for the celebration held in 1905 to commemorate the fourth anniversary of Verdi's death. It was performed in January of 1905 at the Casa di Riposo, a charitable institution to help retired and elderly musicians, and was given a favorable review. The text, in Latin, is from the Roman Catholic liturgy. The work was never published in its entirety.

This music is best sung by mature voices. Notes and rhythmic patterns are not difficult, but the depth and sincerity expressed in the text and music require exact execution of the elements of music. This composition is written for chorus, viola, and organ or harmonium.

STB   Elkan-Vogel 362-03209

Schütz, Heinrich   Wer will uns scheiden von der Liebe Gottes?

As is well known, Schütz composed for a small choir. This composition could be included in the later section on music for the chamber choir, but it can be sung as well by an average size select choir. The music was contained in Part II of *Kleine Geistliche Concerte*, and it is usual to use continuo instruments. Dynamics are terraced and will give no problem to most singers. There is much imitation and duetting between the four voice parts, and these factors, along with the unusual importance of the text, represent the real points to be considered before you decide to perform this composition.

SATB   G. Schirmer 10874

Telemann, Georg P.   **Werfet Panier auf im Lande**

Telemann was a most prolific late Baroque composer whose music is sometimes overlooked. This is an example of the kind of music evoked by troops marching to war accompanied by the music of a military band with trumpet calls. The clear-cut chordal sections and the contrasting imitative portions require a choir with balance throughout. The syllabic setting of repeated eighth notes gives this composition a forthright character that is very attractive. There are no problems here which cannot be solved successfully by a good high school or adult choir.

SATB   Tetro Music Corp. A.B. 102

MUSIC FOR THE FEMALE CHOIR

An increasing repertoire of original music has been composed for the female choir, and today there is less need to rely upon arrangements. The following representative compositions include examples for the various voice combinations and levels of difficulty.

Brahms, Johannes   **Marienlieder**

Brahms composed much music for women to sing while he himself served as the conductor of such a group. The six unaccompanied *Marienlieder* choruses are listed here to represent this large and important body of Brahms' music. One or all six of these choruses will make a fine addition to your library of music for the Christmas season.

These choruses are strophic, and they are capable of being performed by most school and adult choruses. There are no unusual musical problems, and the melodies are typical of Brahms.

SSAA, semi-chorus   E.C. Schirmer 887, 894, 897,
                                                                       886, 895, 885

1. The Angelic Greeting 2. Mary's Journey to Church 3. Mary's Pilgrimage 4. The Hunter 5. Call to Mary 6. Magdalena

Britten, Benjamin (arr.)   **The Sally Gardens**

A simple tune to be sung in unison is here given a fitting and sensitive setting by the one who also composed such well-known choral music as *A Ceremony of Carols*. Of course, this unison song can be sung by virtually any combination of voices, but the recommendation here is to use it with a group of women singers.

Britten was one of the twentieth century's foremost composers, and this simple and natural arrangement serves as a fine introduction to his creativity. This music is especially suited to performance by young singers.

Unison   Boosey & Co. 5448

Jewish Folk Tune   **There Shall Be Peace**

This colorful music is written for women's voices, piano and rhythm section. The ostinato-like rhythmic figure found in all parts in the opening measures builds as the composition progresses; this rhythmic figure serves as the unifying element for the entire composition, and the rhythmic response is infectious. Dynamics for the most part are either soft or loud, and very little subtle response is required. The composition generally is for SSA chorus, but there is some divisi in the first soprano and alto parts. The vocal ranges are well within those commonly accepted, and any choir may enjoy singing this composition for a change of pace and/or for the message of the text.

SSSAA   Lawson-Gould 51958

Monteverdi, Claudio   **Angelus Ad Pastores Ait**

Written to be sung SAA or SAT, the voice parts of this short composition may be doubled by recorders or other suitable instruments. This music is most appropriate for the Christmas season, and it serves as a representative composition from the early Baroque era. The meter moves from duple to triple and returns to duple; each of the three parts is an independent vocal line within the composition as a whole, and the parts enter in imitation. As is true of music of this time, any dynamic markings were added later by an editor. But the terraced dynamics advocated here are in keeping with common practice and such markings may be followed with assurance.

SAA or SAT   Schott & Co. 12

Poulenc, Francis   **Ave Maria**

This composition is taken from the opera, *Dialogues of the Carmelites*, and it was originally written for women's voices. Here is a short piece which requires a mature, yet transparent, sound from the singers. It can serve as interesting concert music, or this music can be used as an introduction to Poulenc's opera. The frequent meter changes reflect the need for flexibility and for more attention to the rhythmic flow of the text than for more usual strictness of presentation. The first sopranos must sing a high "A" softly, but there are no real rhythmic or tessitura problems in this music. Any group capable of capturing the mature, light tone quality required will enjoy performing this brief example of Poulenc's music. Use of the Latin text is recommended.

SSA   Ricordi Mil. 1-3

Verdi, Guiseppe   **Laudi Alla Vergine Maria**

Four Sacred Pieces, composed in 1898, are to be sung by unaccompanied chorus; this composition is the third in the series of four. It is to be sung by boy's or women's voices. The vocal sound required here is the "operatic" sound that we commonly associate with Verdi's music. The lovely and simple chord progression in the opening measures is followed by a short imitative section, and such alternation continues throughout much of the composition.

A large choir of mature and trained voices can make the subtle changes sound without apparent effort and can carry the sound at all required dynamic levels (*f* to *ppp*) to the very conclusion of the composition.

SSAA   Peters 10981

Weelkes, Thomas   **Some Men Desire Spouses**

This is a strophic part-song originally published, 1608, in a collection of *Ayers or Fantastic Spirites* for three voices. The "Fa la la" refrain adds to the humor of the text, and, while each part has some independence, the music is predominantly chordal. There are clear sections in duple and triple meter, and the suggested dynamics appear to be appropriate. This music is not difficult to sing, and the subject matter will have a particular appeal to the young singer.

SSA   Belwin-Mills OCT 2378

MUSIC FOR THE MALE CHOIR

While there are fewer male choirs than other voice combinations, many people agree that there is no vocal sound which surpasses that of a disciplined group of men's voices. These representative compositions show some examples of repertoire for men.

Bartok, Béla   **Five Slovak Folksongs**

One or all of these settings can make fine singing for men, and the text and music is clearly written for mature singers. Meter is not always regular, the first tenors are required to sing a high "A" and you will want to check the requirements of tessitura carefully. In number five, the second tenor part is divided, and this may present a problem if your tenors are not strong.

TTTBB   Boosey & Hawkes 17682

1. Ah, listen now, my comrades 2. Back to fight I'm going now 3. War is in our land now 4. Ah, if I fall in battle 5. Time went on, leave was done

Brahms, Johannes   **Five German Folk Songs**

These compositions are interesting and tuneful, but they are also easily sung. There is some unison and much music for two and three parts, but many of the sections are written for four parts. A chorus capable of singing melodic music in four parts is required. The meter is quite regular, the text is syllabically set, the voice ranges do not place added burdens on the singers, and the phrases are within the average capability of singers. Some or all five of these short compositions will make a fine addition to the repertoire of a young choir.

TTBB   Lawson-Gould 51235

Bruckner, Anton   **Inveni David**

This composition is for four-part chorus and four trombones (ad libitum). The music requires wider ranges than does much music for men's voices, and you will want to check voice ranges carefully. The text is taken from the Psalms, and performance will be best if the chorus is capable of projecting a mature sound at all dynamic levels. Bruckner was well acquainted with the unique timbre of male voices, and particularly effective are the "Alleluias" at the close of this composition.

TTBB   Peters 6318

Handl, Jakob   **O Magnum Mysterium**

Handl, also known as Gallus, worked in Prague after having sung in the court choir at Vienna. He was a sixteenth century composer, and the Reniassance ideal of unity of sound is apparent in his music. Written for two TTBB choirs and continuo, the choirs at times sing together and sometimes are in imitation. The voices generally move in chordal style, and the ranges are usual. You will find this to be an early composition which sounds well.

TTBB-TTBB   Concordia Publishing House
                                                                            98-2270

Spiritual   You'd Better Run

Spirituals are important to the cultural and musical history of the United States, and this composition is one of many. Set for TTBB chorus and baritone solo, this music places special emphasis on natural rhythms. The voice ranges fall well for men's voices, and the chorus adds an interesting contrast behind the baritone solo. Including such compositions as this in your library will provide significant compositions to sing in concert, but will also provide an avenue for acquainting your singers with an important aspect of the American choral heritage.

TTBB/baritone solo   Lawson-Gould 51749

Thompson, Randall   The Last Words of David

Originally performed by the Berkshire Music Center Chorus and the Boston Symphony Orchestra, this music may successfully be sung by a four-part chorus of men's voices, with piano or orchestra. The strong attacks, dramatic changes in dynamics, and accented passages all sound well when interpreted by men's voices. A capable pianist is required, but there are no particularly troublesome musical problems for the singers. Most of the text is set homophonically and syllabically, but there is some imitative treatment in the final section of eighteen measures. The first tenor part requires singers capable of moving to an "A". This composition is also available for mixed chorus.

TTBB   E.C. Schirmer 2154

MUSIC FOR THE CHAMBER CHOIR

The small choir can sing many different types of compositions, and such varied programs as the Christmas feast and the madrigal concert are currently included in usual concert activities. The following compositions are typical of available literature.

Brahms, Johannes   Liebeslieder Waltzer, Op. 52

Melody is always welcomed by concert audiences, and the music of Brahms is known for its melodic content. These waltzes contain bright, interesting music which gives the singer a rich vocal line to sing. The accompaniment is for four hands, and capable pianists are required. A slightly brighter tempo than is indicated will allow the music to flow naturally and freely. All eighteen waltzes may be performed as a major portion of a concert, but, more often, it will be best to select a group of several waltzes much the way a recitalist frequently chooses representative songs from a complete song cycle. While the music will sound best when sung by mature, trained singers, it is within the capability of most serious chamber choirs. This music is said to have originally been performed by a solo quartet.

SATB   Lawson-Gould 834

Carissimi, Giacomo   **Final chorus, Jephthah**

"Plorate Filii" has been a staple in the repertoire for the chamber choir, and the entire oratorio deserves to be considered for performance. Written for six-part chorus, the music itself contains no particular problems. The music is generally homophonic, voice ranges are moderate as is usual in early Baroque music, and the notation presents no particular technical problems. Sung separately or as the final chorus of the complete oratorio, "Plorate Filii" is within the vocal grasp of musically mature chamber choirs in secondary schools or older age groups.

SSAATB   Novello & Co.

Costeley, Guillaume   **Allon, Gay Bergeres**

This sixteenth century French chanson is well-known as a delightful composition for a Christmas concert. Unexpected harmonies provide unusual vocal color, and the intricate rhythmic patterns combine to keep the motion of this short composition interesting at all times. Ranges of voice parts are moderate; the composition is basically homophonic, but there are intricate imitative sections which deserve careful attention. An excellent example of early choral music which is attractive to twentieth century audiences, this composition is difficult and should be performed without accompaniment. The transparent texture will be preserved best when performed by a chamber choir.

SATB   G. Schirmer 10178

Gershwin, George   **The Jolly Tar and the Milkmaid**

George Gershwin is not often considered an important composer of choral music, but this composition possesses a unique delight. The tempo is brisk, and careful attention to the association of clear diction and a clear rhythmic pulse is important. Gershwin himself referred to this music as an English ballad.

There are solo parts not specifically designated, but they are most properly sung by a man's voice and a woman's voice. Diction will present more problems to a medium or large chorus, and the composition will be sung most successfully by soloists or a small chamber group.

SATB   Lawson-Gould 51963

Gibbons, Orlando   The Silver Swan

This is one of two English madrigals to be included in this chapter, and such vocal chamber music can become a major part of your repertoire. The English musician and counter-tenor, Alfred Deller, made a particular study of this music, and his editions are now available for all to use.

While all voice parts generally move homophonically, each must maintain its own vocal line; voice ranges and rhythm should not be problems. This can be a good composition to use in teaching the association of breath support and diction to young singers.

SATTB   G. Schirmer 12043

Hindemith, Paul   Six Chansons

These six settings of French poems by Rainer Maria Rilke are known to most choral conductors, and they should be considered to be standard repertoire for the chamber choir. Hindemith himself is said to have approved the translation into English, and these settings may be sung quite successfully in either the original language or in translation. The use of independent parts, dissonance, precise attacks and releases, and the general transparent character of this music all present real challenges to singers and conductor alike. But they are well worth the time and effort necessary to achieve a high level of performance.

SATB   Schott 10454, 10455, 10456,
                                                             10457, 10458, 10459

1. The Doe 2. A Swan 3. Since all is passing 4. Springtime 5. In Winter 6. Orchard

Jannequin, Clement   Ce moys de may

This is an early example of French choral music taken from *Trente et une Chansons,* 1529, and has a quite simple homophonic setting. Its text is about the joy frequently associated with the month of May. The repetitive and rather simplistic rhythm gives each accented syllable double the value of each unaccented syllable. The music presents no problems, but you may want to use modern French rather than attempt to conquer Renaissance French pronunciation. A modern French version of the text is included with this publication.

SATB   Roger Dean CA-106

Morley, Thomas   **My Bonny Lass**

This madrigal is now known to most musicians, and it deserves to be performed by each new generation of singers. Along with "April is in my Mistress' Face" and "It Was a Lover and His Lass," this composition remains one of Morley's greatest contributions to the English madrigal literature.

This is a two-part strophic composition which uses terraced dynamics, but it presents no real musical problems. The teacher serves more as a vocal coach than as a conductor in the preparation of madrigals, and you are encouraged to present this music seated at a table and with as little visual conducting as practical.

SATB   Harold Flammer 3959

des Près, Josquin   **El Grillo**

A well-known early Renaissance composition, this piece should be included in planning a library of vocal chamber music. This music presents no real musical problems, and it is good for working to develop a fine sense of articulation and ensemble. As is generally the situation in music of this early time, text rhythms, rather than the more recent additions of meter indications, determine the flow of the music and its ultimate interpretation.

SATB   Frank Music Corp. F515

Purcell, Henry   **Choruses from Dido and Aeneas**

This Baroque English opera has often been performed and was originally composed for a girls' school. Most chamber choruses have the possibility of presenting this music in concert or fully staged, for the solo roles are not demanding by twentieth century standards. But a concert performance of several choruses will add much interest to a program of vocal chamber music. The witches choruses, with their "ho, ho, ho" passages, and the final chorus that comments on the death of Dido, represent the great diversity present in this music. Perhaps Edward J. Dent, editor of the Oxford University Press edition, expressed the importance of this work

best when he said: "Since 1895 'Dido and Aeneas' has had several performances, chiefly by amateurs, which have proved that even when represented with the humblest resources Purcell's music has a dramatic poign-
ancy and beauty, which is not surpassed, if indeed it even be equalled,
in the more famous works of Gluck."

SATB or SSA   Oxford University Press

3

How to Maintain
the Choral Library

Maintaining the choral library can be time-consuming, but the well organized library will serve as a valuable resource for you in selecting music for performance. Proper maintainance of the library requires ideas and a few rules clearly set down for all persons to observe. The following discussion includes a comprehensive list of materials that will be useful in organizing and maintaining a choral library of any size. If you are starting to organize a new library, you are encouraged to keep complete records and to observe definite and commonly accepted steps of organization. Your organization should not be complicated, and you can eliminate future problems by using the information contained in this chapter.

ORGANIZING THE LIBRARY

It is necessary for both you and your singers to be able to use the choral library. But you cannot afford to have the music library disrupted because it is available to too many people or because its use is abused. It is possible to set up a system of penalties for abuse of the choral library much as a general public or school library imposes a system of fines for violation of established rules.

The key to encouraging proper student use is to instill in them a sense of pride and respect for their choral music program. It is well known that students will be more careful with music and equipment if they share in the organization of their choir, but no one set of rules or circumstances will work equally well for all situations. Whatever your circumstances, you will be well advised to have the singers themselves, as much as is possible, determine what rules, if any, are to be adopted. Organizing and maintaining the choral library will best be a cooperative project in which the circumstances are such that both you and your singers use the music while also preserving the library for use by future choral musicians.

Card Index File

A good card-filing system is necessary for the efficient handling of a choral library. Careful planning of the filing system can save many hours of time searching for music thought to be in one place but actually found in another location. The file should contain all information you want to know before looking at the music itself. Such information as the following should be included:

1. the number of copies and the date of purchase
2. the title
3. the composer, arranger, and/or editor
4. the voice distribution
5. the accompaniment, if any
6. the library number

You can determine the specific information to be included on each card and then have cards printed or duplicated, or you may obtain commercially prepared cards.

A master index of your choral library may be kept in an ordinary notebook, or specially printed cards may be prepared. If a notebook is used, it is important to use one of such quality that it will remain in good condition over a period of several years. This master index will serve as a quick reference file and should contain the following information:

- library filing number
- correct title
- full name of the composer, arranger, and/or editor
- number of copies on file
- date of purchase

Title Card

The title card has more detailed information, and many conductors and teachers find the title card to be the most used reference source in the card file. Use of the title card permits the information to be listed alphabetically in a file box which accomodates three-by-five-inch or four-by-six-inch cards. The most prominently displayed information is the title of the composition and the library number assigned to that particular music. Quick and easy reference to this information will aid in the efficient use of the card file and ultimate location of the music in the library. The title card may contain almost unlimited information, but selected pertinent facts will usually serve best. Such information should include:

- library filing number
- correct title
- full name of the composer, arranger, and/or editor
- number of copies
- voice distribution of choral and solo voices, if any
- instrumental accompaniment, if any
- publisher
- date of purchase
- date and occasion of performance(s)
- special notes

A filing system may be simple, or it may be complex. If you wish to keep more complete information than will be found on a master index and a file of title cards, you may wish to keep multiple card files. In such a situation, separate files permit the locating of music by voice part, type of music, composer, and any other classification you choose.

Courtesy of J. W. Pepper & Son, Inc.

All information should be kept up to date. If the actual number of copies in the library is less than the number listed in the Card Index File, you will be short of copies when you are ready to hand out music. (Nothing can be more defeating than to have to apologize because the required copies are not available when rehearsals are to begin.) A periodic check of music files and information contained in the Card Index File will keep all records current.

Music Check-Out Card

Records which keep information about music taken from the library will pay dividends over a period of time. Music Check-Out Cards can serve as a very simple device for keeping such accurate records. Organizations that have a copy of all music for each choir member generally will assign a number to each singer (John Jones, No. 1). Each copy of music distributed is given a number, the choir member's folder is given the same number, and that number is also recorded in the master file. But if Music Check-Out Cards are used, they should be similar in size to octavo music and should include the following information:

- name of the school or organization
- brief instructions about how to use the Music Check-Out Card
- library number assigned to the folder and music, if any
- space to show the date taken from the library
- space to show the signature of the person taking the music
- space to show the date returned

An inexpensive number stamp can be obtained from any music or office supply house, and it may be used to stamp the music, the master index, the title card, and the Music Check-Out Card.

STORAGE OF MUSIC

Ideally, you will be able to store choral music in a room adjacent to but separate from the choral rehearsal room. Such an arrangement will allow the music and workroom supplies to be kept away from general traffic patterns, while still being easily used, and all materials can be kept behind a locked door when no one is working in the choral library. Under such circumstances, the music may be stored in boxes on shelves built specially for the purpose. But many physical circumstances do not allow the use of such a special storage room. Frequently the choral library is housed in metal storage cabinets in one part of the rehearsal room.

Storage Cabinets and Boxes

It is important that the choral library be secure at all times; and regular metal filing cabinets with locks make inexpensive, serviceable storage facilities. Specially made boxes or specially printed envelopes are available that will protect music from excessive deterioration in storage, and the use of either boxes or envelopes is recommended rather than the use of ordinary office filing folders. General office folders allow dust to accumulate, and also, our experience has been that copies disappear more frequently when office filing folders are used.

NO. or TITLE

CARL FISCHER
CHORAL FILING ENVELOPE NO. T-4

DATE USED   OCCASION & REMARKS

TITLE _____

COMPOSER/ARR. _____

VOICE ARRANGEMENT _____

EDITION NO. _____

QUANTITY ON HAND _____

CARL FISCHER of CHICAGO

312 S. WABASH AVENUE
CHICAGO, ILL. 60604

Courtesy of Carl Fischer of Chicago

The most recommended storage facilities are boxes in metal cabinets within a room used only for that purpose. But, whatever your facilities, you should store the music vertically rather than simply stacking copies on top of one another on open shelves.

Regular office filing cabinets are not special equipment, and they may frequently be obtained quite reasonably from local office supply houses. Perhaps your school administration has a quantity of office filing cabinets on hand and your music budget may not be charged for this type of equipment. Every few dollars saved in such a way as this will make more funds available for use in purchasing music.

One type of filing box that may be used is that shown below. This box is sturdy, the lid may be purchased separately, and it is easily stored and labelled.

Courtesy of Gamble Company

Gamble's Heavy Board Filing Box

No one storage box or system is being recommended specifically; all equipment shown in this chapter is currently available. You will need to take time to become familiar with different types of storage facilities and then decide what system, or what part of an existing system, serves your needs best.

THE CHORAL FOLDER

Most singers have the use of choral folders, or folios, but there are situations in which you may need to collect all music after each rehearsal. Beginning or general choruses will not learn music more quickly by having the music available for use outside the regularly scheduled rehearsal period. Also, there are choruses that rehearse in sectionals rather than always together, and those groups may use the same music for all sections. In such circumstances, the full choir normally rehearses together only after the music has been well rehearsed and memorized. A skillful choral conductor can bring a choir to a finished level of performance in only a very few rehearsals, particularly if he has also conducted the sectional rehearsals. In such a situation, there will be little need to use choral folders; but this method of rehearsing is not widely used.

In an auditioned choir, each singer usually has a choral folder and is able to take the music for use between rehearsals. This situation has obvious advantages for the mature musician, for the singer may prepare any troublesome musical passages outside the regular rehearsal. If singers take the responsibility for correcting passages on their own time, the scheduled rehearsals will obviously move along more interestingly and efficiently.

Folders for the Choir

As was suggested previously, many conductors use numbered music folders and then match the numbers on the music and folders to the library number assigned to each singer. Any music lost or misplaced can be easily traced, and, under normal circumstances, it is the responsibility of each singer to take care of and return all copies assigned. Some mature choirs use loose-leaf notebooks, and they punch holes in the music so it will be held securely. A few choir directors ask that the bound copies be cut at the fold so there are a series of independent pages that will be free to turn quickly and easily. Other choirs simply punch holes in the music, thus preserving the bound music as it was originally printed.

Choir folders commonly used by singers are of three general types:

1. there are folders with the pockets on the sides
2. there are folders with pockets on the bottom
3. there are folders with elastic cords stretched from posts located at the top and bottom of the folder

While I do not make any single recommendation for your use, several conductors have said that music will be most easily lost out of folders which have pockets at the bottom.

Folder for the Conductor

The conductor's folder deserves special consideration, for it should, at a very minimum, contain all the music and materials you need for your next rehearsal. Frequent apologies to your singers for not having necessary information immediately available will not further your goals. In such circumstances, you will either need to say that you will bring the information to the next rehearsal, or you will disrupt the rehearsal by asking one of your singers to go to your office and find the needed material. Least acceptable is for you to take time to run back to the office during rehearsal to find the information. A properly maintained folder will eliminate problems such as these.

Your folder may be of the same type used by your singers, but under normal circumstances it will be best to use either a three-ring loose-leaf notebook with dividers, or a folder with elastic cords stretched from posts located at the top and bottom of the folder. If the loose-leaf notebook is used, the pages of the music will be free to turn easily and independently. The dividers serve to separate music used for different choirs or concerts. Conductors who work with two or more busy choirs often use a separate folder for each choir, and thus minimize the possibility of error in turning to the wrong music.

MUSIC REPAIR AND DISTRIBUTION

The method you use to distribute music can have an important influence on your singers, and it can either waste time or save time. You should avoid using rehearsal time to distribute music if at all possible. The librarian can easily distribute and collect music after the folders have been placed in the folder cabinet. This method of distribution will cause problems for your librarian if all music folders are not in the folder cabinet when additional music is to be distributed, so you will want to encourage, perhaps require, the singers to leave their folders in place when the librarian is working with the music. While this procedure may inconvenience some singers, it will help your librarian and rehearsal time will be saved.

A music cabinet such as is shown below will be quite helpful in keeping current folders stored in an easily accessible location. You may purchase equipment such as this, or you may have someone make an inexpensive wooden cabinet which will serve the same purpose.

Courtesy of Wenger

Wenger Folio Center

Choral music is given more rigorous physical treatment than is instrumental music, and it frequently requires more repair. You should maintain a particular location, well known to all singers, where they are to place music in need of repair. The music librarian should repair music in current use in order that it may be returned to the performance folder promptly. When music has been performed and is being turned in for storage, all copies should be repaired and any missing copies replaced before the music is returned to permanent storage.

Music Library Equipment

There is standard equipment that your music librarians should have available for use, if they are to be able to work efficiently; the following are among those items:

- Card File Box
- Pens and Pencils
- Paper Cutter
- Rubber Number Stamp and Pad
- Transparent Tape

- Shelves, Tables, or Filing Cabinets
- Sorting Racks

WORKING IN THE CHORAL LIBRARY

The selection of a choral librarian is an important decision, and you will want to give careful thought to this matter. Adult singers normally elect a librarian who is interested and experienced, who is acceptable to the conductor, and who is a member of the chorus. If an election is not held, the conductor will make the necessary arrangements with one of the singers. Younger choirs may elect the person to serve as the librarian, but vocal teachers in secondary schools frequently need to exercise control over the actual selection. It is best to impress the importance of the office upon the singers prior to voting, for a good librarian can make the handling of music quite easy. The choral librarian does need to have an aptitude and skill for such work, and it will be your responsibility to guide young singers in becoming aware of what skills are required of any person.

The Librarian

The duties of the choral librarian include the cataloguing, filing, repairing, checking out, and collecting of all music used. A large choral program may require a different librarian for each chorus, but the library will be maintained best if one person is given the responsibility of supervising all operations. Only by using such structured organization will it be possible to detect quickly the source of any problem which may appear.

The choral librarian is normally paid in a professional chorus, but young students will not often expect pay. However, since this person will spend many hours working in addition to regular rehearsal hours, and since the work of this person can aid considerably in the success of your choral program, your choral librarian deserves some kind of special recognition.

If you use students to work in your choral library, it will be best if you post a notice outlining steps to be followed. The notice may include examples of the most common procedures, or it may be sufficient to list only the major steps to be followed. The maturity, experience, and the length of time each librarian serves will determine just how detailed you should make the instructions you post. But it is generally better to be more detailed than necessary than to not be specific enough for those who need step-by-step direction. Instructions that are over-simplified can be tedious to a degree, but directions that are not detailed enough can be the basic cause of later problems.

A very normal and workable plan is to have one chief librarian with as many assistants as are needed. Each time the office of chief librarian is vacated, it should be understood that the successor will be chosen from those persons who have already worked in the choral library or who have moved from another situation where they have had equivalent experience. While this work is not so complicated that an intelligent person with particular aptitude cannot learn the steps to be followed in a short time, such traits as commitment and punctuality can be determined with much greater certainty when we choose from the group of persons who have already been involved in the work.

CYCLICAL USE OF MUSIC

All compositions included in Chapter 2 are, and most music in your library should be, of such quality as to be useful over a period of several years. Most music ultimately becomes dated, and no one should limit his repertoire entirely to music performed previously. However, much music we have performed previously will be useful again.

It is best not to repeat music performed previously during the same generation of singers. For example, a choir in a high school or college/university will normally wait at least five years to perform a choral composition a second time. This use of your existing choral library makes wise use of funds, all singers can become acquainted with standard monuments in the field, and variety in programming is preserved.

4

Public Performance: Matching Performers and Audience

Making decisions concerning public performance is an integral part of planning for any season in the choral field; this chapter will aid you in making these decisions. Experienced conductors may have already come to a general point of view regarding their own public performance, but we all can profit from constant attention to this aspect of planning the choral season.

PROGRAM BUILDING

Building the concert program is one of the more significant responsibilities of the conductor. While program building is an art, there are many identifiable factors that contribute to the total decision-making process. Just as it is best to know your singers before choosing music to add to your choral library, it is best to know as many specific facts about the performance itself as is possible before outlining the exact music to be sung. In addition to knowing the singers you will use, you should know (1) the type and size of the hall; (2) the type of audience; and (3) the occasion, if it is not to be a formal concert performance.

Every topic discussed in this book touches either directly or indirectly upon public performance. There is much more to consider than merely the actual time of performance in public. But most people, even some choral conductors, look only at that moment when a group of choral musicians bring the total of their background to bear on the performance of a specifically chosen group of compositions for a particular audience. Since some aspect of performing always changes from one concert to the next, we should be aware that any particular interpretation of the music chosen is just that; it is our interpretation on a particular occasion. The background of the conductor and the performers enters into performance, although many more temporary matters may also be encountered in any specific concert. (For example, a soloist may suddenly become ill.)

The composer is a creative musician, but the performer is a recreator. The performer studies the music as completely as is possible, takes into consideration current performance circumstances, and recreates what he interprets to have been the intention of the composer. Because there are, theoretically, an infinite variety of interpretations possible, no two performances are exactly alike. But there are generally accepted limits beyond which no performer or conductor should venture. To a large degree, our study is to learn what those accepted limits are and to remain abreast of changes as they occur; a lifetime of study is required to accomplish this goal.

The actual order of music during a concert can take many different directions, but there are general observations and practices which have often been followed. If we are to know current general practice, we need to know the guidelines most often used.

Four Recommended Guidelines

1. Maintain Unity–Allow Variety

It is useful to maintain unity in program building while also allowing for variety. Our ears are accustomed to an unusual amount of variety when measured by the standards of earlier musical periods. A concert program that is so constructed as to show the evolution of compositional elements in choral music, for example, may not have sufficient variety to hold the interest of a particular audience. At the same time, an audience of choral musicians may rave at a fine performance of the same concert program.

2. Establish Rapport

Many conductors program traditional music of the historical periods during the first half of a concert and move on to different types of compositions, such as folk songs or contemporary music, during the second half. On the other hand, there are situations in which it may be best to establish a rapport with the audience by singing music more acceptable to them first. Again, program building is an art; there is no single set of hard and fast rules that apply to every situation.

3. Use a Central Theme

Most concert programs will be received best if they evolve from a central theme. Christmas programs and concerts built around other important holidays represent some of the most obvious examples of the use of a central theme, but the possibilities are almost inexhaustible. You may wish to build concerts around such themes as:

- American choral music or the music of another country
- Music to show the heritage of different peoples or religions
- Music about work, recreation, love, or death
- Music of one or more of the musical periods
- Music with a contemporary sound
- Music that shows different settings of a particular text, *Ave Maria* for example, or group of texts

Although more choral programs are given by mixed choirs than by male or female choirs, the concert themes listed above apply to programming for any combination of voices. Of course, you may wish to include a group of compositions for male or female voices on a concert program that is predominantly for mixed choir. Such programming will add variety to your repertoire; it will give your men and/or women experience in singing a complete composition or compositions independent of the other sections in your choir; and it will give you an added opportunity to show unusual strengths that may exist in your choir. In addition, the use of accompanying instruments can add contrast and variety to any concert program. But the use of instruments is advocated in particular for concerts given entirely by a female chorus.

4. Consider the Total Impact

You would do well to give consideration to the total impact of the music chosen, after you have taken care to include music that will give your concert programs both variety and unity. We have seen situations where it is useful to choose an opening composition that will give the singers an opportunity to use a full sound without requiring either extreme dynamics or subtle shading. But the total combined impact of all music chosen to be performed on a particular occasion is an equally important consideration. Just as it is possible to be technically correct in performing music and still not actually get to the heart of the music itself, it is possible to observe all the usual rules of programming and still not have a concert program that shows your choir at its best. While there are times when we will want to introduce new music because of a particular interest, we will always want to consider the musical merit of each composition we choose, and the effectiveness of a choral concert will be judged most often in terms of its total impact. Our careful attention to these matters will produce predictable results, and we will profit from the time and energy spent in considering this point.

Four Model Concert Programs

The following concert programs are not presented as being typical, but each is an actual recent concert presented by the particular choir listed. The four examples show repertoire which can be performed by well-trained adult, college/university, and high school choirs, and the listings contain program ideas that are applicable to most choral situations. Although these programs are not shown because they conform exactly to every idea presented in this chapter, your attention is called to the unity, variety, and total impact shown in the music chosen.

---

chicago symphony orchestra

SIR GEORG SOLTI, Music Director
HENRY MAZER, Associate Conductor

86th Season / Chicago Symphony Chorus 20th Anniversary Concert

TUESDAY EVENING, JANUARY 4, 1977, AT 8:00

MARGARET HILLIS, *Conductor*

PHYLLIS BRYN-JULSON, *Soprano*

FLORENCE KOPLEFF, *Contralto*

SETH McCOY, *Tenor*

THOMAS PAUL, *Bass*

CHICAGO SYMPHONY CHORUS,
  MARGARET HILLIS, *Director*

MEMBERS OF THE
CHICAGO SYMPHONY ORCHESTRA

This performance of Bach's Mass in B Minor is dedicated to the memory of Chicago's Mayor Richard J. Daley, who died December 20, 1976.

BACH

MASS IN B MINOR, BWV 232

KYRIE ELEISON

Kyrie eleison .... Chorus
Christe eleison ....Duet, Soprano and Alto
Kyrie eleison .... Chorus

GLORIA

Gloria in excelsis .... Chorus
Laudamus te .. .. Soprano Aria
            Jacques Israelievitch, Violin
Gratias agimus tibi .... Chorus
Domine Deus ... . Duet, Soprano and Tenor
            Walfrid Kujala, Flute
Qui tollis peccata mundi .... Chorus
        Walfrid Kujala, Victoria Graef, Flutes
Qui sedes ad dextram Patris .... Alto Aria
        Grover Schiltz, Oboe d'amore
Quoniam tu solus sanctus .... Bass Aria
        Daniel Gingrich, Horn
    Willard Elliot, Wilbur Simpson, Bassoons
Cum Sancto Spiritu .... Chorus

Kindly refrain from applause until end of concert

INTERMISSION

CREDO (Symbolum Nicenum)

Credo in unum Deum .... Chorus
Patrem omnipotentem .... Chorus
Et in unum Dominum .... Duet, Soprano and Alto
    Richard Kanter, Grover Schiltz, Oboi d'amore
Et incarnatus est .... Chorus
Crucifixus .... Chorus
Et resurrexit .. .. Chorus
Et in Spiritum sanctum .... **Bass Aria**
    Richard Kanter, Grover Schiltz, Oboi d'amore
Confiteor unum baptisma .... Chorus
Et expecto resurrectionem .... **Chorus**

SANCTUS

Sanctus, sanctus, sanctus .... Chorus

OSANNA, BENEDICTUS, AGNUS DEI, DONA NOBIS PACEM

Osanna in excelsis .... Double Chorus
Benedictus .... Tenor Aria
        Walfrid Kujala, Flute
Osanna in excelsis .... Double Chorus
Agnus Dei .... Alto Aria
Dona nobis pacem .... Chorus

Organ continuo for solos realized by Mary Sauer
Organ continuo for Chorus realized by Elizabeth Buccheri

1977 CONCERT SEASON

DANIEL MOE, CONDUCTOR

PROGRAM

I

Cantate Domino . . . . **Earl George**
(b. 1924)

(sung in Latin)

O sing unto the Lord a new song: sing unto the Lord, all the earth. Sing unto the Lord, bless his name; show forth his salvation from day to day. Declare his glory among the heathen, His wonders among all people.

—Psalm 96

A Great Light . . . . **James Fritschel**
(b. 1933)

The people that walked in darkness have seen a great light. They that dwell in the land of the shadow of death, Upon them hath the light shined.

—Isaiah 9:2

Resonet in Laudibus . . . . . **Orlando di Lasso**
(1532-1594)

(sung in Latin)

Resound in praise, O Zion. And with the faithful, joyfully acclaim. He, who was born of Mary, has appeared. Those things are now fulfilled which were predicted by Gabriel. Eija! The Virgin has given birth to God, as divine mercy willed.

Today, born of the Virgin Mary, a king has appeared in Israel.

Great is the name of the Lord, Emmanuel. As it was announced by Gabriel, great is Emmanuel. Eija! The Virgin has given birth to God, as divine mercy willed.

Ave Maria . . . . **Anton Bruckner**
(1824-1896)

(sung in Latin)

Hail, Mary, full of grace. The Lord is with Thee. Thou art blessed among women and blessed is Jesus, the fruit of Thy womb. Holy Mary, Mother of God, pray for us sinners, now and in the hour of our death Amen.

All the Ways of a Man . . . . . **Knut Nystedt**
(b. 1915)

All the ways of a man are pure in his own eyes, but the Lord weighs the spirit. Commit your work unto the Lord, and your plans will be established. The Lord has made everything for its purpose. Yea, even the wicked for the day of trouble. Every one who is arrogant is an abomination to the Lord. Be assured he will not go unpunished. By loyalty and faithfulness iniquity is atoned for, and by the fear of the Lord a man avoids evil. When a man's ways please the Lord, he causes even his enemies to be at peace with him. Better is a little with righteousness than great revenues with injustice. A man's heart devises his way: But the Lord directeth his steps. To get wisdom is better than gold, to get understanding is to be chosen rather than silver. The highway of the upright turns aside from evil. He who guards his way preserveth his life. Pride goes before destruction, and a haughty spirit before a fall. It is better to be of a lowly spirit with the poor than to divide the spoil with the proud. He who handles a matter wisely shall find good. And who so trusteth in the Lord, happy is he!

—Proverbs 16 2-9, 16-20

Offertorium de tempore, K.V. 222 . . . W. A. Mozart
(1756-1791)

Misericordias Domine (sung in Latin)

O Lord, have mercy. We sing to Thee forever.

Quaerite primum regnum Dei, K.V. 86 (73v) . . W. A. Mozart
(sung in Latin)

But seek ye first the Kingdom of God, and his righteousness; and all these things shall be added unto you.

—*Matthew 6: 33*

Litaniae Lauretanae, K.V. 195 . . . W. A. Mozart
(sung in Latin)

Kyrie

Lord, have mercy. Christ, have mercy. Lord, have mercy. O Christ, hear us. O God, the Father in Heaven, have mercy upon us. O God, the Son, redeemer of the world, have mercy upon us. O God, the Holy Ghost, have mercy upon us. O Holy Trinity, one God, have mercy upon us.

CHAMBER ORCHESTRA

Violin I	Violin II
Peter Jaffe	Francine Swartzentruber
Brenda Chieu	Norman Robertson
Lorraine Adel	Kathy Blackwell

Amy Leventhal, Kathy Bickmore, *viola*
Carol Elliott, Roger Heine, *cello*
Beth Orson, Giselle Lautenbach, *oboe*
David Brussel, Kathy Whitelaw, *French horn*
Robert Adair, *bass*

INTERMISSION

III

Four Motets for a time of Penitence . . . Francis Poulenc
(1899-1963)

(sung in Latin)

I. Timor et Tremor

*Fear and trembling have taken hold
of me,
And a heavy darkness descends:
Be merciful to me, O Lord,
For my soul has put its trust in Thee.
Hear my prayer, O God.
Consider my supplication;
For Thou art my refuge and strength.
I call upon Thee, O Lord;
Let me never be confounded.*

II. Vinea mea electa

*My favored vineyeard, I, it was,
who planted you.
Now your sweetness has turned
to bitterness,
Crucifying me and releasing that
Barrabas.
I hedged you in. I took the hard
stones away from your path,
And built a tower of defense.*

III. Tenebrae factae sunt

*Darkness fell upon the earth
When Jesus was crucified.
And abut the ninth hour
Jesus cried out in a loud voice:
My God, why has thou forsaken me?
Bowing his head, he gave up his spirit.
Crying out, Jesus said in a loud voice:
Father, into Thy hands I commend
my spirit.
Bowing his head, he gave up his spirit.*

IV. Tristis est anima mea

*My soul is sorrowful,
Even unto death: stay here and
watch with me.
Soon the angry crowd will close in
on me.
You will run away
and I shall be sacrificed for you.
Behold the hour approaches
and the Son of man is betrayed
into the hands of sinners.*

Three Songs . . . . Felix Mendelssohn
(1809-1847)

(sung in German)

I. Frühlingsfeier

Sweet, golden spring day!
Inner enchantment!
If ever I succeeded in song,
Should it not be today?
Yet why in this season
Should labor begin?
Spring is a noble holiday,
Let me rest and pray.

II. Lerchengesang

What a lovely strain!
O Lark, you raise your song,
It soars joyously.
It takes me from here,
I sing with you,
We climb through the clouds
   to the sun.

III. Herbstlied

Sweet spring, you are past!
Never, never may you stay!
Where I saw your happy flowering
Now blusters Autumn's anxious chase.
How sadly the wind drove
Through the thicket, as it weeping!
Nature's dying sighs
Shudder through the faded groves.
Again—how soon!—
A year has vanished.
Questioning, it whispers through
   the forest:
Has your heart found its happiness?
Rustling woods! Wondrously
Have you touched my heart!
Faithfully, each year brings
New blossom, and new hope.

translation by Marcia Orbison

IV

Te Deum . . . . Joseph Haydn
(1732-1809)

(sung in Latin)

We praise thee, O God. we
acknowledge thee to be the Lord.
All the earth doth worship thee,
the Father everlasting.
To thee all angels cry aloud, the
heavens and all the powers therein,
To thee Cherubim and Seraphim
continually do cry:
Holy, holy, holy, Lord God of Sabaoth.
Heaven and earth are full of the
majesty of thy glory.
The glorious company of the
apostles praise thee,
The goodly fellowship of the
prophets praise thee,
The noble army of martyrs praise thee;
The holy church throughout all the
world doth acknowledge thee
The Father of an infinite majesty,
Thine honorable, true and only Son.
Also the Holy Ghost, the Comforter
Thou art the King of Glory, O Christ,
Thou are the everlasting Son of the Father.
When thou tookest upon thee to
deliver man, thou dids't not abhor
the Virgin's womb.

When thou hads't overcome the
sharpness of death, thou dids't open the
kingdom of heaven to all believers.
Thou sittest at the right hand of
God, in the glory of the Father.
We believe that thou shalt come
to be our judge.
We therefore pray thee, help thy
servants whom thou hast redeemed
with thy precious blood;
Make them to be numbered with thy
saints in glory everlasting.
O Lord, Save thy people and bless
thine heritage.
Govern them and lift them up forever.
Day by day we magnify thee,
And we worship thy name forever
world without end.
Vouchsafe O Lord to keep us this
day without sin.

Have mercy upon us, O Lord.
Let thy mercy lighten upon us,
as our trust is in thee.
O Lord, in thee have I trusted.
Let me never be confounded.

OPTIONAL WORKS

I Wonder as I Wander . . . . . John Jacob Niles, arr.

Ride On, King Jesus . . . . . Robert Shaw, Alice Parker, arr.

Every Time I Feel the Spirit . . . . William Dawson, arr.

Kleine Orgelmesse

by

Franz Joseph Haydn

and

Chichester Psalms

by

Leonard Bernstein

Orchestra
Parkway West High School
Concert Choirs

Kay Ellen Wunder, Soprano
Philip Barker, Soprano

Jerry Anne Galloway

Conductor

Kleine Orgelmesse   Chichester Psalms

by

Franz Joseph Haydn

by

Leonard Bernstein

sung in Latin

sung in Hebrew

Kyrie

I
Psalm 108, verse 2
Psalm 100

Gloria

II
Psalm 23
Philip Barker, soprano
Psalm 2, verses 1-4

Credo

Sanctus

III
Psalm 131
Psalm 133, verse 1

Benedictus

Kay Ellen Wunder, soprano

Incidental Soloists

Kay Ellen Wunder, soprano

Agnus Dei

Jan Harris, mezzo-soprano

Frank Talbert, tenor

Don Diekneite, baritone

THE PRINCETON HIGH SCHOOL CHOIR

in Concert

WILLIAM R. TREGO, *Director*
NANCIANNE B. PARRELLA, *Organist*
GEORGE PETRILLO, *Principal*

JOHANNES BRAHMS (1833-1897)	Ach Arme Welt (Op. 110, No. 2)
ANTON BRUCKNER (1824-1896)	Os Justi Meditabitur Sapientiam
JOHANN CHRISTOPH BACH (1642-1703)	Ich lasse dich nicht Chorale: Dir, Jesu, Gottes Sohn J.S.Bach (1685-1750)
BENJAMIN BRITTEN (1913-1976)	Missa Brevis (Op. 63) Kyrie, Gloria, Sanctus, Agnus Dei
MAURICE DURUFLÉ (1902–)	Motets (Op. 10)

> 1. Ubi Caritas
> 3. Tu es Petrus

MAURICE DURUFLÉ	Organ: Choral varié sur le thème *Veni Creator*
FELIX MENDELSSOHN-BARTHOLDY (1809-1847)	Herr nun lässest (Op. 69, No. 1, 1847)
FELIX MENDELSSOHN-BARTHOLDY	Sechs Sprüche (Op. 79, 1845)

> 1. Weihnachten
> 2. Am Neujahrstage
> 6. Am Charfreitage

BENJAMIN BRITTEN	Rejoice in the Lamb (Op. 30)

Amy Ford, *soprano*   Randy Thompson, *tenor*
Katherine Hilst, *alto*   Miles Pratt, *bass*

Sunday, March 27, 1977, 5:00 p.m.

THE EVANGELICAL LUTHERAN CHURCH OF THE HOLY TRINITY

Central Park West at 65th Street, New York, New York - A. James Laughlin, Jr., Pastor

Physical Characteristics

You should be very practical in building a choral program. In taking into account the hall and the audience, you will want to also be considerate of those to whom you will sing. But you will not want to give the appearance of "singing down" to any audience. For example, a concert of madrigals sung in a large hall can hardly be as successful as the same concert would be when sung in a small hall. We are not discussing the use of different and less difficult music to gain acceptance by an audience, but we are saying that the size of the hall, its acoustical properties, and other similar physical matters play an important part in determining what music will be received best. This may be a particularly difficult problem on tour, for there is no way to prepare as specifically when we are dealing with several different halls in unfamiliar circumstances. In such instances, we will want to test the acoustics in the hall before beginning the concert. Choirs that tour with a repertoire extensive enough to sing two or three different concert programs can select the specific program to more nearly take advantage of the actual physical properties encountered. Of course, the use of choral risers and a shell will help to keep acoustical variation to a minimum.

THE PERFORMERS

A concert will be received best if there is a match of the performers and audience. But many of us err in giving more consideration to the audience than we give to our singers. While it is true that the singers, too, will want to present a concert program that will please the audience, we conductors and teachers should also keep in mind that we have an added responsibility to our performers. We may enjoy presenting "shows," but a steady repertoire limited to "show" music will not expose our singers to enough different types of music to aid their full musical development.

Now Is The Time To Execute

A successful conductor knows that musical performance will be at its best when musical, psychological, and physical preparation are brought to a peak at the same time. To omit or to minimize the importance of any one of these factors is to bring your choir to a performance without full preparation. This book is devoted to a discussion of various facets of total preparation of the music, but the psychological and physical aspects of preparation for performance should also be given importance.

We are all aware that a singer performs best when he has a sense of well-being. If there is nervousness for any reason, the sound will have a tendency to be less full because the singers "tighten up." When this happens, a multitude of musical and vocal problems may appear. Increased self-assurance comes with performing, but it is important that even the youngest performer knows before he steps on stage that he is fully prepared to deliver the music programmed. Under such circumstances, the concert will have a strong beginning, and the performer(s) will respond increasingly to the acceptance by the audience as the concert progresses. The total concert experience is communication through choral music; both audience and performers participate, and proper preparation will aid in assuring success.

Preparation for Singing

The importance of the physical body to the singing process is equally well known. There are books that deal primarily with this aspect of performance. But we shall here discuss briefly the single most important physical consideration in choral singing—the use of the breath. The basic principles involved in the use of the breath need to be understood by everyone who performs or coaches others who sing. If you are not satisfied that you know how to teach your singers to use the breath efficiently, it will be helpful if you will attend workshops, do some reading on the subject, and/or discuss the subject with voice teachers.

Use of the Breath

A basic part of properly sustaining vocal tone is to utilize proper physical control. This control becomes more difficult as we grow older because our muscles are no longer as capable of responding to subtle variations asked for in the music. The increasing lack of muscular response frequently makes it impossible for an older singer to sustain a vocal phrase as long or as successfully as he/she could have several years before.

Since the support of the breath, or "singing on the breath" as it is sometimes referred to, is so very basic to the production of mature vocal sound, the careful and full understanding of this point is well worth the time and effort required.

A choral conductor who does not understand vocal technique is handicapped almost as severely as is a conductor who has had little or no training in such areas as music notation. Proper execution in each area is necessary if we are to prepare our singers well, and to omit proper vocal training is to advocate the maintaining of the status quo rather than to train the singers to produce a more mature vocal sound.

Many of us remember a time when there was thought to be a conflict between solo singing and choral singing. It is hoped that we now understand that the production of a free vocal tone will serve the soloist as well as the choral singer. Singers will perform most naturally if they:

1. observe good posture, with the head tending upward by stretching slightly, the chin tucked in, the shoulders down, and the chest expanded
2. inhale with the chest held high while remaining still
3. exhale through the lips while keeping the chest held high

Singers who have difficulty in doing this may find it helpful to observe the functioning of their diaphragmatic muscles when:

1. sitting on a chair
2. leaning forward with the elbows on their knees
3. taking large breaths

What we are discussing here may be summarized as:

1. supporting the breath from the diaphragm
2. careful and simultaneous starting of the breath and vocal tone
3. consistent sustaining of the vocal tone throughout the musical phrase
4. finishing the vocal sound at the conclusion of the musical phrase
5. taking another breath from the diaphragm
6. repeating this total process for each and every musical phrase sung

These steps can be taught to any of our singers, and the sound of our choirs will improve just because of improvement in the use of this technique.

Singing: A Point of View

We should not try to say that singing is only a physical or an intellectual process. The learning of languages and the understanding of the music we perform depends primarily upon academic information, but physical responses such as are being discussed here are just as important a part of training the successful singer. The proper use of the body cannot be overlooked if we are to prepare singers fully for musical performance.

Those of us who teach in schools, in particular, have a two dimensional responsibility. When we decide what music to include in concert programs for a season, or for the period of time that a student will be a member of our choral program, we determine the depth and breadth of the music that particular student will know best. While too much responsibility should not be placed on any one teacher, it is a fact that we make major decisions about the musical education of those students who sing in our choirs when we choose the music they will perform. It should be emphasized that, while we must always consider the audience, we will be better teachers if we also give a high priority to performing music that will contribute to the musical growth of our students.

THE AUDIENCE

There is no doubt that we should take the audience into account when we choose music for performance. Although we may sometimes sing primarily for the parents, relatives, and friends of our singers, even they will find it difficult to sit through an entire concert of music that is outside their general level of understanding. An audience that has little or no personal acquaintance with those who are performing will more often show even less personal tolerance, and some audiences may attend a concert only to judge the musical performance from a critical point of view. Even then, of course, the background of the listener plays an important part in his reaction to the particular music being performed. For example, two equally qualified musicians may differ significantly when asked to evaluate a performer's use of ornamentation in music of the Baroque era.

Musical Understanding and the Consumer

The choral conductor who deliberately sets out to educate audiences in the same way that he works to educate his singers will either find the music programmed to be too esoteric for the average audience or not sufficiently challenging for the performers. Generally, there are at least two different levels of musical understanding present at a performance, and it is necessary for you to anticipate such differences before the concert actually begins. Also, the occasion frequently determines audience receptivity to the particular music programmed. For example, a full concert of sacred music may be well received when sung in a church or at a chapel service, but that same music may be out of place when sung for an occasion such as a festive banquet. We all have our ideas about what music is appropriate for a particular occasion, and many in the audience will be confused if the music performed departs greatly from what they had expected. Only when singing for the most knowledgeable and critical audiences may we expect to have the performance evaluated primarily in terms of the music itself, and even then we may find considerable variation in the responses of different people.

It is important that a rapport be established between the audience and performers as early in the concert as is possible. As has been said, it is often best to begin a concert with a full, direct composition that will show the full sound of the choir, but that will require relatively little subtle response from either the performers or the audience. Such a composition will make it relatively easy for the singers to begin singing in the concert and it will also give the audience an opportunity to begin to focus attention on the concert itself, after having had to spend a period of time waiting for the concert to begin. An audience will usually only feel the necessity of sitting quietly before the music begins when the concert is given in a church; in any other setting the audience needs to hear a first composition which will aid them in bringing their attention to the concert itself.

We may have a concert program which utilizes only a single choral work, but there are relatively few unaccompanied choral works which last even as long as one hour. When we think of programming a single work on a choral concert, we almost always turn to such oratorios as *Messiah*. Although such concerts occur with some regularity, it is safe to say that most choral concerts include more than one composition.

A concert program that includes two or more compositions should be given considerable thought, for the overall succession of music is important. Any time we allow our audiences to be confused or disturbed by the succession of the music we program, we leave ourselves open to the criticism of those who do not understand our thinking.

While a concert performance of an oratorio may take as long as several hours, the usual program should not exceed an hour-and-a-half of actual music. Many concerts include music that takes only about one hour to perform. The exact length is not so important as is the fact that it is better to leave the audience wanting to hear more music than for you to have sung so long that the audience is exhausted.

Not only is it generally best to select music that has a common theme or subject, but it is important to consider the matter of key relationship between compositions. A full concert of music in the same key, or a succession of compositions in totally unrelated keys will not be considered good program building. Such concerts will tend to leave the audience either bored or confused. It is important, then, that we consider the eighteen criteria listed in Chapter 1, but it is equally important that we give careful thought to a theme, to key relationship, and to related matters when we are deciding in what order the music is to be performed.

The Performance Itself

It is necessary for us to realize that at the moment of performance we need to rise above those individual matters that take so much of our time and attention during rehearsal. When we begin a concert we are immediately involved in trying to communicate an ideal sound which recreates the composer's ideas as nearly as possible as the concert progresses. If we have chosen the music well, the concert will contain music to which we and our singers have a commitment. If we have prepared the singers and music carefully, we can give our undivided attention to transmitting the best our singers have to offer. Real communication will result, and this is the final important challenge of musical performance.

PART TWO

SCORE PREPARATION

5

Score Preparation
and the Rehearsal:
Guidelines and Models

The major topic to be discussed in this chapter will be score preparation, a subject which gets too little attention outside classes in music theory. This topic is useful for preparing performance music itself, and it is not to be considered just an academic exercise of limited practical value. Increased attention to preparation of the choral score should not replace any other area of rehearsal preparation. With more score study will come more complete understanding of the music, and depth of musical understanding will further enhance musical performance.

We will discuss matters that are best addressed before rehearsals begin, and those topics include specific acquaintance with your singers and the musical score. We shall not be able to go into great detail about rehearsal technique itself because of limited space. But some of the more significant matters are applicable to any study in this area.

APPROACHES TO REHEARSING

The audience only hears music as it is performed in public; the actual choral experience for the performers is to be found in the rehearsal. Public performance affords the opportunity to communicate musical insights identified and brought to the understanding of the performers during rehearsal.

In almost every instance, it is best to read a composition from beginning to end when the music is first handed out. On any first reading, you should make reasonable allowance for mistakes. Your chorus should first hear their own singing of the composition as a whole, even if the first reading is far from the performance level expected ultimately. After this first reading has taken place, you should begin to work specifically toward mastering notation in the most technically difficult portions of the score.

A pattern of rehearsing in which you always begin by singing the first measures of a composition is to be avoided, for sections at the conclusion will thus be neglected. Those sections which will require less rehearsal time can be brought into the schedule as the more difficult sections begin to take shape. In this way, the entire composition will reach performance level with a minimum of repetition. The use of such a general rehearsal procedure will enable you to make an efficient use of rehearsal time, but care should be taken not to dwell on a particularly difficult passage too long at any one rehearsal. Briefly, the advantages of using this plan may be summarized as follows:

- Difficult sections will be given the most time and attention from the very beginning.
- Less difficult sections will be given sufficient, but not too much, rehearsal time.

Planning in this way will achieve the following results:

- You will not have the anxiety of being uncertain if the entire composition will be ready when the concert date arrives.
- Individual sections and the total musical score both become clear and meaningful.
- Rehearsal time is used efficiently.
- Performance level singing is achieved with a minimum of drill and with maximum understanding.

A comprehensive time table for rehearsing a composition will be well-received by your singers, and valuable rehearsal time will be used more wisely if you have estimated in advance the time required to perfect each aspect of the composition. While your schedule may need to be revised from time to time as you progress toward a concert date, you should not allow the need for making changes to keep you from approaching a season with such a comprehensive time table to use as a basis for working.

Refining Musical Rhythm

The execution of musical rhythm and the accompanying speech rhythm is one of the most fundamental matters to be considered in the choral rehearsal. Speech and the text will be discussed in Chapter 7, but some of the more basic aspects to be considered in isolating the elements of musical rhythm will be discussed briefly at this time. It should be understood, however, that space does not permit a complete treatment of the subject.

Rhythmic training should begin at the earliest possible moment. Imitation of invented rhythmic patterns, and/or patterns taken from music being rehearsed, can serve as valuable training for even your youngest singers, and the use of this technique will always be helpful in clearing up particularly difficult rhythmic passages. In younger singers, this technique will be useful for building general rhythmic response or for clearing up a particular passage; more mature choirs will find the technique more confined to use in correcting troublesome rhythmic passages in music being rehearsed.

Basically, this approach involves a leader and a group of followers. In the simplest of terms, the conductor claps to represent a series of notes and the chorus imitates the pattern. The use of several patterns of varied difficulty will quickly determine the level at which the singers need to work; at some point, one or more choir members will clap late and further work should proceed from that point. It is best not to explain more than is absolutely necessary, for you are working to achieve a refined, natural rhythmic response. Too much mental involvement frequently will create errors, for the person who consciously counts and claps must coordinate two responses. Complicating the process in this manner makes these experiences unnecessarily difficult. We are dealing with what is essentially a natural gift, and too much mechanical teaching may only lead to unnecessary problems. For example, the following pattern can be imitated by almost everyone on the first hearing.

To take time to discuss quarter notes, eighth notes, accents, and related topics only complicates what is ordinarily a very simple and natural response. After your choir is proficient in responding to intricate rhythmic patterns by clapping, you may wish to expand your verbal discussion of troublesome notational elements. But to mix what is ordinarily a physical response with learned information is only to complicate the problem unnecessarily.

This technique is useful in working out a particularly difficult section in music being rehearsed, and you can use this discussion as a basis for making your own exercises to correct specific problems encountered by your singers. The following examples contain more complex patterns which require more careful responses, but, again, these patterns are intended only to serve as a point of departure for your work.

You may wish to divide your choir in two, three, or four groups and let the different groups alternate in responding. One group may respond on counts one and three while the second group responds on counts two and four; group one may respond in measure one and group two then respond in measure two. If your choir is experienced at working with this type of exercise, or if your singers enjoy a challenge, you may wish to divide your choir into two or more groups with each group clapping different rhythmic patterns at the same time. Of course, you may vary these exercises by using different parts of the body.

SCORE PREPARATION BY THE CHORAL CONDUCTOR

It is of fundamental importance for the choral conductor to prepare the music before it is passed out for rehearsal, but there should also be additional preparation before each new rehearsal. The following remarks are presented to aid in that preparation, but there is no thought to giving a complete analysis of the music chosen.[1]

Your preparation of the musical score involves many stages of study. Here is a list of several of the most important points:

- Determine the overall form of the music. Test your memory by making a broad outline such as is included for the three compositions discussed in this chapter.

---

[1]See for further information: Decker, Harold and Herford, Julius (eds.), *Choral Conducting: A Symposium* (Englewood Cliffs, [N. J.]: Prentice-Hall, Inc., 1973), pp. 177-230.

- Determine the essential details as they relate to the movement of the music. Again, test your memory by filling in essential details section by section.
- Sing and/or play the vocal and instrumental parts for firsthand acquaintance with musical and performance characteristics.

Study of several compositions by a composer will give us a better understanding of the specific composition chosen for performance. Also, knowledge of the characteristics of the musical period, and study of a composer's works within that context, will give us a more sound basis for in-depth study of the music to be performed.

The following pages include specific comments about three very different compositions. The three works were chosen to show an octavo composition, a composition which is largely instrumental, and a large choral composition. These selections were chosen to represent types of compositions, rather than as specific recommendations for your choir to perform. They may serve as models of effective score preparation.

Ives: Sixty-Seventh Psalm[2]

This composition is an early example of Ives' use of bitonality, g minor for the tenors and basses and C major for the sopranos and altos. While the use of two keys is unmistakable, Ives stressed that they were to be thought of as one unified whole. The composition is essentially in three parts as far as the association with the text is concerned; measures one to fifteen include verses one to three, measures sixteen to twenty-six include verses four and five, and measures twenty-seven to thirty-five include verses six and seven of the psalm text.

Section one is harmonically a series of triads, one juxtaposed on the other. The resulting progression emphasizes C major in the upper voices, and is supported by a melodic line based upon C. Beginning at section two, there is imitation which alternates between the men's and women's voices. Ives leads to a half cadence at measure twenty-two, which is followed by a brief quote from section one. The last section generally repeats the substance of section one. While there is some rhythmic change because of the new text, Ives repeats the chord structure and melodic line of the first six measures. Verse seven uses bitonal chords that first appeared in section one, and the final chord progression forms a I-IV-I cadence.

Perhaps the one observation about the music that should be kept in

---

[2]Musical references have been taken from the Associated Music Publishers publication number A-274.

mind is that Ives intended this composition to be looked upon as one large chant.

1	15	16	22	23	26	27	35
C		Ascending line:		Measures		General repeat	C
g		F		23-26 equal		of several	g
		Descending line		measures		measures in	
		suggests: b flat		12-15.		section one.	
						I-IV-I cadence	
						formula.	

Beethoven: Symphony No. 9, Op. 125[3] (Fourth Movement)

Beethoven's Symphony No. 9 is a work which needs no introduction; most of us have performed the work and studied it in class. Its unique place in music history is cited for reasons which include the use of voices in what was known to be strictly an instrumental form, and the work has served as a model for generations of students, performers, and composers. Since this work is performed regularly by virtually every symphony orchestra and chorus, it seems fitting that the fourth movement should be chosen for discussion and analysis.

Beethoven composed his ninth symphony during his last period, but there is evidence that shows he had intended to set Schiller's text many years before. At the time he had been working on his seventh and eighth symphonies and had made some decisions about the ninth, but he had no idea of including this text in a choral symphony. The actual content of the ninth remained to be worked out as the project progressed.

There is an introduction of ninety-one measures, but the movement is basically a series of eight variations based on the following theme.

Following the theme and variations, there is a magnificent double fugue.

---

[3]Musical references have been taken from the Eulenburg Miniature Score, No. 411.

Introduction

1																					594
1																					330
1																					91
1	8	9	16	17	24	25	29	30	37	38	47	48	55	56	62	63	64	65	76	77	80	81	91

3 Presto
4

d ff

1st recit. — 2nd recit. — 3rd recit. — 4th recit. — 5th recit. — 1st mention of theme — 6th recit.

1												594
1												330
92												207
92	115	116	139	140	163	164	187	188	191	192		207

Theme in unison — Variation one — Variation two — Variation three — Coda to variation three

Allegro assai

1												594
1												330
208												240
208	216	217	219, 220, 221	223	224	229, 230, 231	236	237				240

Presto

Baritone solo begins

Solo baritone part related to earlier 'cello recitative

Variation Four – Variation five – Variation six

241	264	265	268	269	292	293	296	297	320	321	324	325		594
Variation Four		Coda		Variation five		Coda		Variation six		Coda				

1 _____ 594

1 _____ 330

241 _____ 330

241 _____ 330

Stanza I   Stanza II   Stanza III

Introduction

342	343	350	351	358	359	366	367
	A¹		A²		B		A²

1 _____ 594

331 _____ 594

331 _____ 374

331 _____ 374

Introduction

B flat

Variation seven: 331-431

375	382	383	390	391	398	399	406	407	414	415	422	423	430, 431
A¹		A²		B		A²		B		A²		Coda	

1 _____ 594

331 _____ 594

375 _____ 431

375 _____ 423   430, 431

Stanza IV

92

Double Fugato

1													594
331													594
431 Double Fugato													454
431	434	435	438	439	440	441	444	445	448	449	452	453	454

II:2nd Vl,Cl I:1st Vl
I:Fg,Vc,Cb II:Vla

I:2nd Vl
II:Vla,Ob

II: 1st Vl, Ob, Fl
I:Vla,Vc

Modulate to various keys
Rhythm for theme II is taken from variation VII

1											594
331											594
455											488
455	458	459	462	463	468	469	476	477	484	485	488

II:1st Vl
I:Fg,Vla,Vc

Modulate to various keys

1											594
331											594
489											516
489	490	491	492	493	496	497	502	503	508	509	516
b					e						

Ascending bass

Modulation using rhythms from the two themes,
but taken primarily from the first theme of
the double fugato

93

Top diagram:

1													594
331													594
517													542
517	524	525	528	529	530	531	534	535	536	537	540	541	542
	Begin F sharp octave			Ob,Fg suggest theme				Ob,Fg suggest theme				Strings pre- pare for variation eight	

Bottom diagram:

1												594
331												594
543												594
543	550	551	558	559	566	567	574	575	582	583	590	591	594
A¹		A²		B		A²		B		A²			Coda

Variation eight: 543-594

The reeds essentially double the chorus

Stanza I

595 ————————————————————————————————————— 762

595 ———————— 602 | 603 ——————————————————————— 654 | 654

595	602	603	610	611	618	619	626	627	630	631	638	639	646	647	654
Second theme		Repeat second theme				Signature change to one flat									

Andante Maestoso

3
2

G

Chorus of Stanza I

595 ————————————————————————————————————— 762

655 Double Fugue ——————————————————————————— 729

655	662	663	670	671	678	679	686	687	692	693	700	701	708	709	719	720	729
I:Soprano		I:Bass		I:Tenor		I:Alto				I:Soprano						I:Alto	
II:Alto		II:Tenor		II:Bass		II:Soprano				II:Alto						II:Bass	
Subject First entry		Answer Second Entry		Subject Third Entry		Answer Fourth Entry				Fifth Entry						Sixth Entry	

Fugue subject in tonic, answer in dominant

I: uses stanza I

II: Uses chorus of stanza I

595 ·· 762

730 ·· 762

730　733　734　737　738　741　742　746　747　750　751　754　755　758　759　762

Bass-chorus　Tenor-chorus　Alto-chorus　Full chorus

Stanza III

Measure 758: Controversial C natural

763 ·· 940

763 ·· 842

763 ·· 813

763　772　773　782　783　794　795　806　807　809　810　813

Allegro ma non tanto　Soloists enter　Chorus enters Full orchestra and soloists　Poco adagio

Alla breve

Stanza I: First four lines, then second four lines

763 ·· 940

763 ·· 842

814 ·· 842

814　817　818　821　822　831　832　840　841　842

Tempo I　Poco Adagio　Bass drops to A

Stanza I continued

763														940
843														940
843	846	847	850	851	860	861	868	869	876	877	879	880	886 887	894

Poco allegro
V1 and lower
strings repeat
drop from B
to A

Prestissimo
Alla breve
Coda-material
taken from
second theme

763										940
843										940
895	907	908	915	916	919	920	927	928	935 936	940

ff

Continue full
orchestra and
chorus

Maestoso

3 ff
4

Overlap into
measure 920

Chorus concludes

Prestissimo

4 ff
4

J. S. Bach: St. John Passion[4]

The *St. John Passion* was first performed on Good Friday of 1723; it was composed in Cöthen and first performed in Leipzig, just a short time before Bach was officially appointed to go to Leipzig. The libretto was taken from St. Matthew and St. John in the *New Testament*, and Brockes' text. In contrast to the *St. Matthew Passion*, this work requires only a single choir and the choruses are not on such a large scale.

Because of the length of this work, attention here will be given only to selected portions. But, while recognizing the importance of analytical study, we should not overlook the emotional impact of the work as a whole. In the *St. John Passion*, Bach does not hesitate to mention the spiteful actions of the enemies, and, therefore, the choruses of the crowd play an important part in the story. While this is music of Bach and its introspective nature is apparent, emotion is also present.

Number One – Chorus

At the beginning of this chorus, the organ and continuo maintain the pedal bass while the violins introduce a subject consisting primarily of groups of sixteenth notes in thirds. The flutes and oboes introduce what is often referred to as a theme of woe, and beginning in measure nineteen the chorus acclaims the Almighty. At measure thirty-three, the mood changes further as the sixteenth note figure is passed to the organ and continuo; a fugal theme is introduced by the basses and is taken up in turn by the tenor, alto, and soprano sections.

The phrase shown below is begun by the basses in measure fifty-eight and is subsequently taken up by the tenors, altos, and sopranos. It is close to the "Crucify" theme in Number Fifty-Nine of the *St. Matthew Passion*.

As the chorus progresses, the theme of woe as originally expressed in the woodwinds now recedes while that of the strings swells increasingly. The chorus joins this theme at measure seventy in a tutti passage marked *forte*, the fullest dynamic marking used in the entire opening chorus.

---

[4]Musical references have been taken from the Eulenburg Miniature Score, No. 965.

1				A				𝄐 58
								Fine
1	18	19		32	33		39	40	58
g									g

The first eighteen measures are
    essentially repeated three times.
Text: abbcca

58				B				95
								Da Capo
58	66	66	70	70	78	78	86	86	95
E flat									D

Number Thirteen – Soprano

This aria does not follow the usual procedure of answering the preceding recitative, for the recitative refers to Simon Peter while the aria is sung
by a soprano. The text is original rather than Biblical, and it gives the
impression of confidence which almost surely was not Peter's state of mind.

1	16	17		A		48	49		B		112
Opening ritornello		17	40	41	48	49		66	66	78	79	112
			B flat F	Central				g	Medial			d
				ritornello					ritornello			
Text: abbcca											

113		A¹		156	157		164
B flat		Medial ritornello		B flat		Closing ritornello	B flat

Numbers Sixty-Seven and Sixty Eight – Chorus

The burial portion begins with the recitative of the Evangelist in
Number Sixty-Six and also contains these two choruses. Bach used descending figures to describe the lowering of Jesus' body into the grave, and
an example of this figure is shown below.

The two funeral choruses in the *St. John Passion* and the *St. Matthew Passion* are alike in both tonality and measure. The funeral chorus of the *St. John Passion*, however, is smaller than that of the *St. Matthew Passion*, and it is felt that this may be the reason that the *St. John Passion* concludes with this magnificant chorale.

1			A				60
1	12	13	32	33	48	49	60
Opening ritornello						Closing ritornello	
61	B¹	72	73		A		112
113	B²	124 D.S.	13		A		60

No. 67

1	2		4	7	(7)	9	11
(11)	13		15		16	18	21

The type of study discussed in this chapter does not present easy and quick answers, but it does present a means for developing a deep understanding of the music you perform. This area of study is one of the most often neglected, and mastery of the type of subject matter presented here will inevitably further enhance the level of musicianship exhibited by your choirs.

6

Preparation
of the Choral Score:
Performance Practices

The relationship of the choral score and performance is a very large subject and it is important that we give it increased attention. While a complete discussion would take more space than is here available, we can comment on important aspects of the topic.

Numerous extensive and reliable historical studies in the field of choral music have only recently been available. Since time does not permit most performers to engage in their own original research, there is room for more writing by those who are acquainted with research tools, who believe it important to perform music as close as possible to the composer's original intention, and who are themselves experienced choral musicians.

There have been basic differences in the performance of choral music in various periods of music history, and it is of fundamental importance that we be informed of the characteristics that were present and which influenced each period. But this will not be primarily an historical discussion. We shall be interested in those topics which will benefit you most in preparing music for performance by your choirs.

PERFORMANCE OF RENAISSANCE CHORAL MUSIC

The Renaissance (c. 1450-1600) is the most recent musical period in which vocal music was clearly dominant. Vocal music of that time was often sung by soloists and many compositions were suitable for performance either by soloists or a small choir. The music itself most often consisted either of a single line chant, or it was a polyphonic composition in which the voices interacted contrapuntally. Conducting singers generally was accomplished with a minimum of motion given by the lead singer. These signals usually consisted of visually reminding the singers of the inflections in the melody and the broad direction of the music. Such indications were given by using a circular motion of the hand. When the music was strict and more complex, conducting ordinarily consisted of a vertical up and down motion of the hand, a small stick, or a roll of paper to indicate the normal pulse. But there was no attempt at communicating more refined musical shading. There was no thought of utilizing a conductor who would have given his entire attention to the performers as does the conductor today.

Books in the field of music history already contain extensive discussions of recognized musical forms, and it does not appear to be helpful to duplicate such information here. But it may be helpful in a general way to know that, when we perform choral music of the Renaissance, we are essentially performing a mass, motet, chorale, anthem, chanson, or madrigal.[1] Less often discussed are topics that deal more specifically with choral performance itself, and these are the subjects that will receive our primary attention.

It will be helpful to keep in mind that the Renaissance composer often supervised the performance of his own music, and the composer frequently conducted the rehearsals and performance. There was much closer personal supervision by the composer than is common today, for wider distribution of music has now made more performances possible over a wider geographic area. Today's composer normally can supervise only the most prestigious performances, and, even then, his authority is limited. Since this aspect of performance supervision is quite different today than it was during the Renaissance, there is now greater need for more specific written instructions for the performers to follow,

Choral Singing and Vocal Quality

The voice quality used today differs from the vocal quality prevalent during the Renaissance, and our approach to Renaissance choral music will be most valid if we are acquainted with the basic conditions that existed at that time. Three important differences in choral performance appear when

---

[1]See for further information: Ulrich, Homer. *A Survey of Choral Music.* (N.Y.: Harcourt Brace Jovanovich, Inc., 1973)

we compare practice in the twentieth century to practice during the Renaissance:

1. The Use of Women Singers
2. Vocal Quality
3. The Size of the Ensemble

The Use of Women Singers

While the most common voice combination now is to use both men and women, choral music in the Renaissance essentially used men and/or boys. Because of this basic difference in common practice, it is difficult today to duplicate the use of male voices in all voice ranges, and an exact duplication may not be desirable. While there is little doubt that there were differences in sound between their male sopranos and altos and our female sopranos and altos, we should accept the fact that it is not possible to duplicate exactly the vocal timbre originally used in music of this time. Countertenors give the closest comparable tone quality, but, of course, countertenors are not generally available. Women singers are commonly used for performing the soprano and alto parts, and it appears to be more practical to continue to work with this arrangement than to seriously question the use of women singers.

Vocal Quality

Evidence about the use of tone quality is contained in such sources as their written word, paintings and sculpture, and it appears that the vocal production of individual singers during the Renaissance was more rigid and tense than that of today. Under such circumstances, it is normal for a more strident and nasal vocal sound to result. Also, it is generally understood that little or no vibrato was used in ensemble singing. It is recommended that little, if any, vibrato be used now by singers when performing polyphonic choral music, for wide vibrato will tend to blur individual vocal lines. But to recommend the use of a "straight" tone is not to imply that singers should use a sound which lacks vitality. Any performance will be received best when a vital sound is projected.

The Size of the Ensemble

In most instances, the size of choirs now is larger than the size of choirs used most often during the Renaissance. During the fifteenth and sixteenth centuries, choral ensembles generally numbered from less than ten singers, in the earlier years, to about thirty; but there are individual recorded examples of ensembles which numbered more than two times that number. The Papal choir of the sixteenth century is reported to have numbered about twenty-four singers. Sacred music was sung by such a choir, while secular music, such as the chanson and madrigal, was considered either to be solo music or to utilize one singer on a part.

There is considerable evidence which shows approximately one dozen men and boys to have been grouped around a lectern holding a single partbook. Secular partbooks were smaller, and this, too, would appear to support the view that sixteenth-century secular music was performed by quite small ensembles.

Rhythm and Tempo

While these topics may be of as much general concern to music editors as to performers, there are points in both areas that will make a performance more valid if incorporated.

Today, our system of notation is based on the proportion of one to two—a whole note equals two half notes. During the Renaissance, the proportion was either one to two or one to three; for example, one longa could equal two or three breves. Only when the values were smaller than the minim were they in double proportion. This system was freer than that of earlier times, and it opened a whole array of new possibilities for rhythmic development.

Tempo is a consideration that directly contributes to the success of a choral performance, and tempo is determined by the conductor. The problem is complicated by the fact that no clear direction is given in original scores. Since few examples of tempo markings have been found, we must assume that young performers during the Renaissance first became acquainted with common practice by performing with more experienced musicians. Tempo considerations were important to composers and performers, but we should realize that the composer ordinarily was present for rehearsals and performance. Also, the idea of a variable tempo is essentially a modern concept.

Tactus, the complete down-up motion used by the conductor, is a term which applies here; it refers to a fundamental tempo. Variability of tempo was practically unknown; when a change in tempo was called for, the desired result was achieved by a change in the tactus. While tempo was more constant in choral music of the Reanissance than it is today, scholars often do not agree on the exact tempo best suited to performance of a particular composition. However, there is evidence to support the conclusion of Gustave Reese who stated that 60 to 80 semibreves per minute were generally most accurate.

The Use of Instruments

Influence of the unaccompanied style most exemplified by Palestrina remains strong to this day, but we should also understand that instruments were often used. While there are differences in practice as shown in the vocal and instrumental music of the Baroque and later times, no such clear distinction existed in the Renaissance. During this period there was one practice.

When we realize that instruments were often used in vocal music of the Renaissance, we immediately open up more possibilities for our own performance. As is common knowledge, instruments used during the fifteenth and sixteenth centuries had a very different sound than do instruments commonly used today. If it is possible to use authentic instruments, reconstructions of instruments used originally, then you will be well advised to use such existing original instruments. But if we are concerned with matters of real authenticity, we should also investigate such matters as pitch. Very few situations allow sufficient time, staff, and funds necessary to research every detail of original performance. Since we generally cannot investigate all matters that concern original performance, we must select those areas that are of most concern. But it is recommended that modern instruments be used if no reproductions are available. Of course, modern instruments should be chosen which are as close in sound as possible to the originals.

When we perform music that uses both voices and instruments, or two or more choirs, we should give particular consideration to the placement of the performing groups. The most often cited example of this type of music being performed during the Renaissance referred to the association of the Gabrielis at St. Marks Basilica, Venice. Two or more groups were used and they were placed opposite one another; the performing groups were separated sufficiently to insure clarity in performing each separate line.

PERFORMANCE OF BAROQUE CHORAL MUSIC

The Baroque era (1600-1750) is the age in which the use of instruments and singers together became the rule; it is the age in which female sopranos and altos began with some regularity to replace male sopranos and altos in choral singing; it is the age in which more than one musical practice emerged; it is the age in which the traditional dominance of vocal music was challenged by instrumental forms; and it is the age in which there came to be much fuller expression of a single emotion or mood.

The conductor as we know him today is not a part of performance practices during the Baroque era. But the focus moved from the previous practice of the lead singer using a vertical motion with a small stick, a roll of paper, or the hand, to the keyboard performer, who visually gave the most important directions while performing the continuo part at the harpsichord or organ. Not always did musicians agree on the specific patterns to be used with a particular meter. But a series of patterns used at the close of this period has been documented by Marpurg in *Anleitung zum praktischen Musik überhaupt* and *Anleitung zum Clavierspielen*. His patterns were taken from Italian, French, and German sources, and representative patterns appear below.[2]

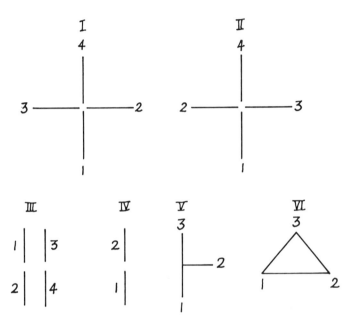

Distinguishing characteristics of French, Italian, and German music became more clearly defined during the Baroque era. Such performance guides as ornaments and figured bass symbols were more often written out in French music than in Italian music. And, of course, J. S. Bach was influenced by the music of Italian and French composers as well as by previous German composers. Along with these distinctions in national styles, there existed two compositional practices:

1. *prima prattica*, first practice—utilized polyphony, traditional text setting, modality, and some rhythms

2. *seconda prattica*, second practice—utilized tonality, homophony, the principle of affection, and more intricate rhythmic structure

[2]Georg Schünemann. *Geschichte des Dirigens*. (Leipzig: Breitkopf und Härtel, 1913), pp. 148-49.

Since the conductor now presided at the keyboard, his attention was divided between conducting the ensemble and his own realization of the figured bass. The size of the ensemble was still generally small, by later standards, and the need for a conductor who gave his total attention to that function was not as great as it came to be during the nineteenth and twentieth centuries. Also, the conductor was still usually a composer. He was either performing his own music, or he was often performing the music of contemporaries, whose works he may have edited or changed to suit his own purposes.

There were large choral festival performances in Germany and England, and those which included the music of Händel have been very influential. But such performances were exceptions when compared to usual Baroque practice. Festival performances frequently utilized hundreds of performers and, at times, two or more conductors. These were spectacular events. The added problem of communication because of the large number of performers involved was one characteristic of performance that influenced the movement toward utilizing a full-time conductor, as is the custom today. Schünemann shows the following examples of a performance layout when singers and instruments are required:[3]

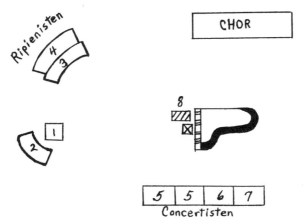

1. Cello ; 2. Bass ; 3 Streicher ; 4. Bläser ; 5. Konzert violine ; 6. Flöte
7. Cello ; 8 Gesang solo.

Realizations of the figured bass have normally been written out in published performing editions, and most performers now simply use the edition as published. But, you may realize the bass yourself.

---

[3]Ibid., p. 186.

Ornamentation

The place of ornamentation in music of the Baroque era is one of the most difficult subjects to comprehend, because musicians are now trained primarily in common practice of the nineteenth and twentieth centuries. The use of ornamentation was expected during the Baroque era. Ornamentation was sometimes written, but it was simply understood in other instances. While it is not possible to discuss every situation, there are guidelines that will be helpful in working out your approach to these problems. Some of the more important guidelines are:

- Ornaments may be written fully, partially, or not at all.
- Parts for high instruments ordinarily include more ornamentation than do parts for low instruments.
- When the continuo utilizes a harpsichord, more ornamentation may be appropriate than when another instrument is used.
- Solo portions normally contain more ornamentation than do portions performed by the choir.
- Each new piece of music should be looked upon as an individual and separate problem.
- An ornament may be performed instead of, or in addition to, that note in the melody to which it is most closely related.

Unresolved questions concerning the use of ornaments have proven to provide real problems, and rather than take a chance on making wrong choices we have often simply performed the music strictly according to the printed page. It is important to realize that ornamentation was originally expected in this music; when performing without ornaments, we are actually omitting what was considered to be an integral part of the composition. While it is not possible to give definite examples that always apply, the following are among those most accepted.[4]

Groppo

[4]The following examples have been taken from: (1) Aldrich, Putnam, *The Principle Agréments of the 17th and 18th Centuries: A Study in Musical Ornamentation* (Cambridge, [Mass.]: Harvard University Press, 1942); (2) Dannreuther, Edward, *Musical Ornamentation* (N.Y.: Edwin F. Kalmus, n.d.); (3) Dolmetsch, Arnold, *The Interpretation of the Music of the XVII and XVIII Centuries* (London: Novello and Co., 1946).

Mordent

Appoggiatura

Appoggiatura

Trill

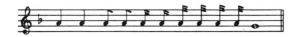

Turn

Cadence Détachée

Cadence Détachée

Choral Singing and Vocal Quality

Staggered breathing was practiced during the Baroque era, just as it is used now. It was important enough for Praetorius to include in his list of vocal vices to be avoided. Many authorities commented on the use of breath, saying the singer should neither take a breath too often nor in the middle of a word.

It is evident that more constricted and strident singing was present in the Baroque era, just as it had been present during the Renaissance. Johann Mattheson took a disrespectful attitude toward German singers, comparing them unfavorably with their Italian and French contemporaries. According to him, German teachers did not seem to care if the voice came from the throat or was obstructed by the position of the tongue. Marpurg advocated a way of singing that was essentially in agreement with the way singing is now taught; writings such as Marpurg's document the transition from older practice to methods more commonly used at this time.

Most writers acknowledge the use of two registers: head and chest. But the falsetto was also cultivated, and falsettists were frequently used to sing soprano and alto parts. Those teachers who advocated using the falsetto gave much attention to the difficulty of changing from the natural voice to the falsetto.

Choral singers were either men, women and/or boys, or men and women. While castrati were very important to the development of opera, boys, women and/or falsettists were used to perform the soprano and alto parts in choral music. As the use of women singers increased, the practice of using the falsetto declined. For this period of transition, there are recorded examples of male and female altos singing the same part in the same range and at the same time. Today, high men's voices, called countertenors, may be used, but women's voices are most commonly employed to perform the soprano and alto parts. While large groups of performers were sometimes used in open air performances, small to medium-sized groups are more appropriate to usual performances of Baroque music.

The Use of Instruments

We generally use instruments when we perform Baroque choral music. Instruments were classified in two general groups:

1. ornamental, those whose purpose it was to ornament and vary the melody
2. fundamental, those used to support the harmony

Certain instruments were capable of performing in either class, and such instruments could be used for color as well as for realizing the figured bass. There is no doubt that considerable skill was required of those who played ornamental instruments as well as of those who performed with the figured bass as their basis. Those who played instruments in the higher ranges were expected to be especially proficient at improvisation, although some improvisation was expected of those who performed both types of instruments.

Modern performances of Baroque music often have omitted the use of instruments, and this misconception may have been a carryover of the performance of unaccompanied sacred music of the Renaissance. The use of instruments is appropriate in this music, and this part of a performance can become a major problem. If we have authentic instruments available and the performers to play them satisfactorily, then our problems are limited to selecting the proper combination of instruments. But, if authentic instruments are not available, more difficult choices are necessary. The substitution of a 'cello for a gamba to double the bass line of the continuo part is certainly possible. But to substitute the use of a piano for the preferred harpsichord is quite a different matter. While we prefer the use of authentic instruments if at all possible, we do not see the lack of these instruments as sufficient reason to avoid all performance of this music. If it is necessary to use a piano, for example, ordinarily it will be best not to try to give the impression that the performance is an attempt to recreate the sound as it would have originally been heard.

Notation: Pitch and Rhythm

Pitch and rhythm evolved according to modern conventions during the Baroque era, but many examples of old practice remained during the seventeenth century. Key signatures in early Baroque music were often used to indicate a transposition of mode: (1) one flat indicated a transposition down a perfect fifth, and (2) two flats indicated a transposition down two perfect fifths. This type of signature is often called a partial signature, and matters of pitch were generally more carefully notated in late Baroque music than in earlier Baroque music.

The interpretation of rhythm in Baroque music is difficult to discuss in exact terms, for there was variation according to such influences as country and type of composition. The general observation is that the performer should adhere to using the rhythm as shown on the printed page and depart from the printed notation only if he can justify such departure on the basis of clearly documented evidence. But there are instances when we should not interpret the printed page strictly. The following examples are among the most common relationships to be found:

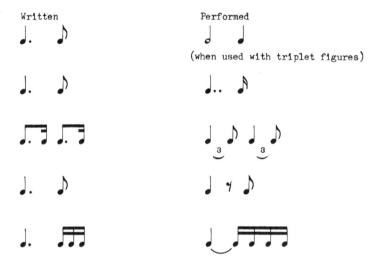

While usual dynamic change involved terracing, there are recorded examples where more subtle dynamic shadings were called for in the music.

PERFORMANCE OF CLASSIC CHORAL MUSIC

It was during the Classic period (c. 1775-1820) that the conductor took his place beside the composer and the performer, and it was during this time that polyphony of the late Baroque gave way to a predominantly homophonic style. Rather than emphasizing the bass line, emphasis was placed more heavily upon the soprano line, and that part was supported more equally by all the other voices. Since the continuo generally was no longer to be considered a factor in the musical score, the keyboard performer was usually not the one who conducted. This position ordinarily became the responsibility of the concertmaster, but, in choral music, the organist continued to divide his attention between conducting and performing.

Any careful study of the Classic period should evolve around the music of Haydn, Mozart, and early Beethoven, and this is the period in which most major musical forms for orchestra took their place in the repertoire. Characteristics most associated with the music of this time include increased objectivity, clarity, restraint, symmetry, and delineation of form. These are relative terms which are used to describe general characteristics of late eighteenth century and early nineteenth century music as contrasted with music of earlier and/or later times. While there were several decades of experimentation and transition between the Baroque and Classic periods, often called the Rococo (c. 1725-1775), choral music produced during this time is not sufficiently significant in today's performing repertoire to be included in the present study. It should be mentioned, however, that this time period included many years during which William Billings was active in the United States.

Essentially, the musician of the Classic period was in the employ of artistocracy. He composed music for court occasions, and he was employed for the prestige that his creations could give his patron. Aristocratic expression and manner were formalized; conduct emphasized courtly manners; and art music reflected this more elegant, reserved, and objective approach.

Voices and Instruments

Matters concerning the proper use of voices and instruments in choral music of the Classic period are easier to determine than for earlier periods. Instrumentation was more clearly recorded in the score, and those instruments called for are generally in common use today. While Baroque choral works (with the exception of such works as Handel's *Messiah*) most often use a small chorus and instrumental ensemble, choral music of the Classic period more often uses a larger chorus and a smaller instrumental ensemble. This is the period in which both the chorus and the instrumental ensemble generally became larger, but a work such as an early mass of Mozart is still not well-suited to performance by a large ensemble.

Voice production and instrumental performance practices began to approximate those current in performance today. For example, modern valved trumpets can be used to perform parts originally written for trumpets with no valves. But the use of the continuo is less widely understood.

While the continuo was no longer present in most music, opera and church music were the last to give up this practice. Much choral music of this period still included the continuo, and this point may be confirmed by observing the figures under the bass part in the score. Its use is not as pronounced as during the Baroque era, for the instrumenation is now more carefully designated. But the continuo part is to be included in performances of many choral compositions of the Classic period. Including the continuo in a performance today, where appropriate, will add clarity of articulation. Since the continuo is no longer the central part in the instrumental ensemble, the keyboard performer will best concentrate on adding clarity of rhythm while maintaining the posture of an ensemble performer. There should be no attempt to assign a major role to the continuo; rather, volume should be compatible with the ensemble as a whole, and any added ornamentation should be kept within the scope appropriate to that particular ensemble.

Rhythm and Tempo

Music of the Classic period was lighter and more delicate than music of the Baroque. Baroque music basically moves by beats, and music of the Classic period generally moves by bars. Tempo also was moderate in music of the Classic period, and extremes were to be avoided. Directions regarding meter and tempo were more often included in the score during the Classic period. Italian terms such as *allegro* and *moderato* were commonly used as were signs to indicate dynamic changes. While all previous observations are to be taken into consideration, it is also important to maintain sufficient clarity and crispness to insure an interesting performance.

Tempo rubato is discussed in the writings of C.P.E. Bach and Mozart, and it is clearly to be considered when interpreting music of this time. It is reasonable to assume that other composers and performers knew of this interpretive device, but it is recommended that *tempo rubato* be used with discretion when performing music of the Classic period. The use of *tempo rubato* means that the melody may be performed with some rubato while the accompanying parts are performed in strict tempo. Its use was more pronounced in the Romantic period, and we will be well advised to avoid exaggeration in the use of *tempo rubato* when performing music of the Classic period.

Ornamentation and Improvisation

The use of ornaments and improvisation is not a matter of such great importance to music of the Classic period as it is when we perform music of the Baroque or Renaissance. No longer does the composer allow the performer to use his discretion to the extent that was the custom during earlier periods. Of the three major composers whose music is included in the Classic period – Haydn, Mozart, and early Beethoven – surely it is Beethoven who would have been most offended if performers had added to the music as written in the score. Mozart's operas represent a musical form where ornamentation persisted, and it appears that both he and Haydn may have been open to some addition by the performer. But it appears that any such addition would be most appropriate in arias of extended works. Since it is known that the continuo was still utilized in much choral music of the time, this part allowed for some element of discretion by the performer. But improvisation was no longer basic to choral performance as it had been during the Baroque era. Its use was almost always confined to such special new situations in instrumental music as a cadenza in a concerto.

There are problems of ornamentation when some choral works of this period are performed, and, to some extent, the point of view taken will depend upon whether the conductor follows the thoughts of writers like J. Quantz, C.P.E. Bach, and Leopold Mozart, or the later Spohr, Hummel, and Czerny. You will want to study these practices in detail when you perform music in which ornamentation is appropriate, but the observation is that rules of the late Baroque era are most often to be followed.

Expression

One of the most important means of expression is the use of dynamics, for there was a move to include the *crescendo-decrescendo*. This development was in major contrast to the earlier use of terraced dynamics in the Baroque era. While the *crescendo-desrescendo* was not entirely unknown before the Classic period, the work of Stamitz at Mannheim was most notable; for practical purposes, its use was not a major performance consideration before the time now being discussed. The use of *crescendo-descrescendo* when performing choral music of the Classic period is to be treated with restraint. The *crescendo* should not begin at as low a level nor move to as high a level as it may in music of the Romantic period or the twentieth century. Of course, the *descrescendo* is to be treated in the same manner.

The practice of performing identical, successive musical phrases at contrasting dynamic levels is a point to be considered in the Classic period. Briefly, if the portion is first performed *piano*, the repetition will be performed *forte*; if the portion is first performed *forte*, the repetition of the music will be performed *piano*.

In summary, the composer of the Classic period worked toward simplicity and lightness of texture in his music. He avoided extremes as shown in later works, and unity of structure was more important than emotional content. Polyphony was not as important as it had been during the Baroque era, and now the inner voices assumed greater importance. Previous emphasis on the outer voices now gave way to an emphasis on the soprano part while the bass line interacted with the inner parts.

PERFORMANCE OF ROMANTIC CHORAL MUSIC

The Romantic period (c. 1820-1900) is not to be confused with the use of the term "romanticism" as applied more generally. The former describes characteristics present in compositions of approximately the last eighty years of the nineteenth century while the term romanticism describes factors to be considered in a performance of the music of any period. This discussion will concentrate on the most significant factors to be taken into consideration when performing the music of the Romantic period. While there is not sufficient space to enter into a detailed discussion of this point, we will interpret the Romantic period as beginning with the later works of Beethoven.

Voices and Instruments

This is the period in which the human voice was first used in the symphony, and Beethoven's Ninth Symphony remains one of the most often performed works. No longer is there the problem of working with instruments or performance forces that are not now commonly employed. We now find music that requires a large number of singers as well as compositions for chamber chorus. Since the orchestra has been greatly enlarged, it is essential that singers put out more sound when performing with an orchestra in a work of this period. The size of the chorus will ordinarily be larger than the orchestra; the exact number of singers will vary depending on their vocal capability, but the number ordinarily will not be more than two times the number in the orchestra.

Rhythm and Tempo

Rhythm and tempo became less strict than during the Classic period, and there were less frequent changes than were to come in the twentieth century. But the effect of changes in meter without changing the signature was achieved by displacing accents. The Romantic composers achieved the appearance of changing meter by using irregular rhythmic accents; a twentieth century composer would more often change meter signatures.

Tempos of the Romantic period were not as restrained as they had been during the Classic period; a slow tempo was often performed quite slow and a fast tempo frequently was performed very fast. Abrupt changes of tempo were now more common, and the actual tempo generally was influenced by the mood of the composition. *Tempo rubato* was more often employed and was used more fully. *Ritardando* and *accelerando* were used more effectively than during the Classic period.

While there is different use of rhythm and tempo by composers of previous periods, individuality is much more evident in the choral music of this time. While it is important to study the music of individual composers in any period, because of this greater difference in the Romantic period it is now necessary more than ever in order to make accurate judgments about the use of the various devices in the specific composition(s) being performed.

Expression

In choral music, as in other areas, the Romantic period was the time when performance was most personal in nature. Dynamics and other means of expression were at their height, and the performer was freer to include considerable personal opinion in performance interpretation. A wider range of dynamics was found, and there was more prominent use of extremes. Dynamics ranging from *ppp* to *fff* were often used, and there are recorded examples often outside these limits.

Crescendo and *descrescendo* became widely used during the nineteenth century. At times there was gradual dynamic movement from full to soft or soft to full, but there were also instances of such movement occurring quite abruptly. The use of dynamic accents, such as *sforzando* (*sfz*), occurred more frequently and added to dynamic possibilities. (See Beethoven, Symphony No. 9, fourth movement.) There are also terms such as *andante maestoso* (moderately slow, flowing, and majestic), which include directions for both tempo and dynamics.

This increased range of expressive devices available to the performer gives greater freedom but also includes added responsibility, particularly for the conductor. For example, along with the added possibility of attaining greater variety and contrast, the conductor must now study the music to be performed so that he can decide upon and maintain proper pacing. Unfortunately, some conductors substitute an emphasis on simple dynamic effect for a well-read interpretation. Such questions as how full to make a *forte*, or what does *andante maestoso* really mean, are of particular importance when we conduct this music.

Harmonic possibilities within tonality were explored more fully during the Romantic period, and there was a growing tendency to use chromaticism. This is the period of the very large performing ensemble, but there is also considerable repertoire for the chamber choir. The music more often is homophonic and a full, mature vocal sound is needed. There is increased use of irregular phrases and cadences are often more obscure.

Every new musical period is brought into existence because of a major reaction or revolt against the major characteristics of the previous period. Composers of the Romantic period reacted against the formal structure adhered to by composers of the Classic period. Now, unusual rhythmic and harmonic effects, wider use of dynamic levels, and less regular phrase structure are usual. Tone color is a most important consideration, and the lyricism of the human voice is to be taken into consideration when performing any music of this period.

PERFORMANCE OF TWENTIETH CENTURY CHORAL MUSIC

Late in the nineteenth century, many divergent styles of composition began to emerge. Such terms as post-romanticism, impressionism, neo-classicism, twelve-tone, aleatory, and electronic have been used to identify directions taken, and many of these styles and techniques are represented in the field of choral music. Examples taken from representative compositions will be included in Chapter 11, but a comprehensive discussion of each style is outside the scope of the present study. Books and articles, some of which are listed at the close of this chapter, are available for more detailed examination of all styles and techniques which have significantly influenced the direction of music in the twentieth century. This discussion is directed toward more unique matters which influence choral performance.

Basically, techniques used in this century have either moved toward more control or toward more freedom in the performance of music; twelve-tone is an example of the use of more control, and aleatory, "chance," is an example of a technique which incorporates greater freedom. Sacred choral music follows the usual posture of ordinarily being more conservative than secular music.

Voices and Instruments

Any problems that appear in twentieth-century music because the composer has asked for specific voices and instruments appear because the composer has asked for performing forces to produce a non-traditional sound. Problems related to the use of old instruments and voice combinations have been replaced by new considerations. Twentieth-century composers ask for a variety of sounds that singers may sometimes call unmusical and/or not conducive to proper voice production. These sounds may include shouts, whispers, tongue clicks, hissing sounds, and/or the use of an unnatural production to achieve a whole range of non-traditional vocal sounds. Timbre is frequently more important in non-traditional music than is directed toward more unique matters which influence choral performance.

Rhythm and Tempo

Rhythm, as used in music of the twentieth century, is varied and often complex. There frequently are intricate rhythmic patterns and meter changes, and there is much variety of rhythmic groupings and accents. Generalizations are difficult since this music includes the rhythmic vagueness found in Impressionism, rhythmic expression as found in non-traditional notation, and numerous directions between.

Tempo, like rhythm, is related directly to the text and style of the specific composition being studied. Tempo changes in twentieth-century music are frequently abrupt, and greater skill frequently is required of the conductor. Scores are now marked more carefully by composers, and metronomic markings are frequently included. Of course, you are well advised to use metronomic markings as a guide rather than relying on a strict adherence to those markings in the score. But these indications in the music do serve as a valuable guide to the performer.

There are twentieth-century compositions that require instruments and singers to perform in two or more tempi simultaneously. In such circumstances, the preferred situation ordinarily is to use a different conductor for each group. Also, there are sections where free tempo prevails, and such sections may be either noted verbally or by the composer including boxes or brackets to enclose the particular sections in the score. Once again, matters of rhythm and tempo to be considered preliminary to performance are related directly to the text and the style of the specific composition being studied. Directions included in the score can be valuable to the conductor when determining how to appropriately interpret the music being considered for performance.

Expression

While Impressionistic music utilizes relatively subtle dynamic change, twentieth-century music generally requires a more extreme dynamic range than does music of the Romantic period. Composers often include many and varied dynamic effects such as rapid *crescendos* and *decrescendos*, accents, and extreme dynamic contrasts. Choral singers of today who sing extensively may expect at some time to perform music which requires usual vocal sounds but also such sounds as yelling, whispering, tongue clicks, and hissing. One sings "blue notes" in jazz, and common practice includes ornamentation and improvisation. Since there is little written instruction in this field, perhaps the best way to begin to learn is to listen to recordings by such great performers as Ella Fitzgerald.

Texture in twentieth-century music is also quite varied; there are such techniques as ninth and eleventh chords used within major-minor tonality, whole tone, and twelve tone. Texture is often more complex, and there is increased use of counterpoint as compared to the previous century.

Twentieth-century music includes a wide variety of musical styles. While specific terms, such as neo-classic, are generally used to identify composers who use particular techniques, it is often difficult or impossible to make such definite statements. Therefore, it is of particular importance to study individual scores or the works of a particular composer, if we are to achieve our best understanding of the music we perform. Our continued goal is to acquire knowledge that will help us in making decisions about what general information applies to a particular composition and what information does not apply. Then, we can use the general information as a basis for becoming more specifically acquainted with the music we perform.

RECOMMENDED FURTHER READING

Aldrich, Putnam. *The Principle Agréments of the 17th and 18th Centuries: A Study in Musical Ornamentation.* Cambridge, [Mass.]: Harvard University Press, 1942.

Arnold, Frank T. *The Art of Accompaniment from a Thorough-Bass.* N.Y.: Dover Publishing Co., 1965, 2 vols.

Bukofzer, Manfred F. *Music in the Baroque Era.* N.Y.: W.W. Norton & Co., Inc., 1947.

Dart, Thurston. *The Interpretation of Music.* London: Hutchinson and Co., Ltd., 1954.

Dolmetsch, Arnold. *The Interpretation of the Music of the XVIIth & XVIIIth Centuries.* London: Novello and Co., 1946.

Dorian, Frederick. *The History of Music in Performance.* N.Y.: W.W. Norton & Co., Inc., 1966.

Reese, Gustave. *Music in the Renaissance.* Revised Edition. N.Y.: W.W. Norton & Co., Inc., 1959.

Rosen, Charles. *The Classical Style.* N.Y.: W.W. Norton & Co., Inc., 1972.

Ulrich, Homer, and Pisk, Paul A. *A History of Music and Musical Style.* N.Y.: Harcourt, Brace & World, Inc., 1963.

7

Analyzing the Choral Text

Vocal music always includes text as well as music, and choral musicians are sometimes guilty of paying too little attention to the text. Since our training is primarily within the field of music, it is only natural that we should think first about the music. But the choral text also deserves careful attention, and we shall discuss the text in this chapter.

Books frequently have been more concerned with such matters as diction and language. But this chapter will be concerned with matters important to the setting and performing of the text; the text is our third major point to be considered in score preparation.

Although the text is important to all vocal music, it is of special significance in music for the chamber choir. Since it would take several chapters to discuss this subject thoroughly, the present discussion will be limited to repertoire suitable for performance by madrigal singers or the chamber choir. Only by approaching the subject in this manner will it be possible to avoid simply dealing in generalizations that may be appropriate but may not be sufficiently close to the subject matter to be most helpful. This chapter, then, will be devoted to discussing aspects of the choral text as they appear in the English madrigal.

English madrigals are among our most often performed choral compositions, and every one of us would be well advised to consider including examples from this repertoire in the music performed by our chamber choirs. This music is widely appreciated by musicians and audiences alike, and in the United States it presents no added problem of learning another language. While this music is known to most choral conductors, it is recommended that you give careful thought to performing it, especially if your singers have not had the experience of performing madrigals.

THE TEXT AND VOCAL SOUND

Before entering into a discussion of matters that relate more specifically to text as poetry, it is appropriate to deal briefly with the matter of the text and the sung tone. Solo singers normally work with elements involved in a full understanding and performance of text more than do choral singers. If your singers have studied and performed solo repertoire, they will more nearly understand the importance of this topic. If your singers have not had such vocal background, it would be helpful to include comments about this in your rehearsal schedule at appropriate moments.

It is generally known that singers sing with the emphasis on vowels, and a part of score preparation and rehearsing is to recognize and perfect the sound of your choir on the vowels found in the music. Most of us use exercises and warm-ups that include working with this aspect of vocal sound, but we more often may not give sufficient attention to the meter of the text. Words have stressed and unstressed sounds just as music has accented and unaccented beats. If the composer has been sufficiently sensitive to the text, the metrical considerations of music and text will coincide. But it appears that we are too often willing to accept the fact that the composer should have given careful attention to this point; we may not examine this relationship of text and music sufficiently to acquaint ourselves firsthand with specific details in the music we perform. It will be time well spent for you and your singers to systematically go through the score identifying vowel sounds and vocal techniques to be used where there may be some indecision by your singers.

Consonants, too, are important to vocal sound. If we are fully acquainted with the proper vocal handling of consonants, we can then more nearly transmit this information to our singers. But, once again, this aspect of vocal training will generally be more carefully studied in the studio of a teacher of singing.

While the above paragraphs outline briefly how training will be most thorough, if we do not have the aid of private teachers and diction coaches we can do much to help our singers ourselves. A thorough knowledge of phonetic sounds and the placement of consonants can give basic information that can be applied in a great number of situations, and, again, there are books on these subjects. One reference source that many singers and conductors have found quite helpful is *The Singer's Manual of English*

Diction.[1] This book may contain more information than is needed for your choir, but it is a reference that can be consulted for answers to most phonetic problems.

THE SUITABILITY OF A TEXT

It is no new departure to say that there is a real kinship between text and music; one hardly needs more proof than is to be found by hearing such music as Gibbons' "The Silver Swan." The music of the Gibbons song, for example, is effective even when heard without the text, but the text is of such quality that a hearing of text and music together makes the hearer realize that the total work of art is greater than either element alone.

Music and text have elements in common; they each have sound and they each have rhythms. The careful union of these two elements is basic to mature performance, and, under normal circumstances, this union is most clearly shown in performances by chamber choirs. To examine this union of music and text, the following points should be observed.

- The singers should learn to deal with both music and speech (phonetic sounds).
- Careful study of the text will add to the emotional and imaginative content of performances by your choir.
- The union of music and speech can normally be most carefully communicated when one or only a few voices are involved.

In order to achieve an acquaintance with the text that will make such a level of communication possible:

- You should read the text aloud several times before you decide to include the composition in your performing repertoire.
- Your singers should scan the full text with special attention being given to the most difficult portions; this will give the greatest possible understanding of the text being sung, and it will provide in-depth knowledge of the audible sound characteristic and the singer's own physical feeling.

Let us consider one brief example that illustrates the point that music and text can best complement one another; the following example is an excerpt from the alto part of "Arise, Awake" by Thomas Morley as taken from *The Triumphs of Oriana*.

---

[1]Marshall, Madeleine. *The Singer's Manual of English Diction* (N.Y.: G. Schirmer, Inc.).

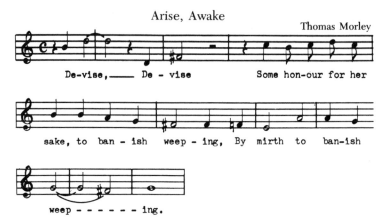

The text in the example shown above is only a portion of the poem, but in the context of the poetry it is without any great emotional importance. Morley increased the importance of "Devise" by the use of repetition and by sustaining the second syllable on a higher pitch. He set "some honour for her" in short notes so that "sake" stands out as the most important word of that phrase. Then he gave the line a slowly descending passage to a longer and lower note for the first syllable of "weeping." The line continues to descend chromatically to another half-note on "mirth" and the mood of "weeping" is sustained. "To banish weeping" is repeated, and now "weeping" is made even more dramatic by being set to much longer notes and by being placed at the cadence. Morley's setting adds to the dramatic quality and importance of the original poem; both text and music add to the expressive quality.

Many poets, whose texts have been included in this music, have remained anonymous, for it was not the custom for a composer to give credit to the poet when he published his madrigal or ayre. But, at least one composer was also active as a poet. Thomas Campion was a lyricist of first rank and an important composer as well; he set some of his own poems to music, but Philip Rosseter is known in particular for his settings of Campion's poems.

THE POEM AND THE SETTING

Since the poetry is produced first and has an important influence on the music, it is of basic importance to give more specific attention to the text and its setting. "The Match That's Made" by William Byrd and taken from his *Psalms, Sonnets, and Songs of Sadness and Pietie,* 1588, gives information about the music of Byrd, as well as about the English madrigal text. A portion of the text is as follows:

The match that's made for just and true respects,
  With evenness both of years and parentage,
Of force must bring forth many good effects,
    Pari jugo dulcis tractus.

For where chaste love and liking sets the plant,
  And concord waters with a firm good will,
Of no good thing can there be any want.
    Pari jugo dulcis tractus.

While there are six stanzas in all, this music, like many other madrigals, has only the first stanza printed with the music. The remaining verses are printed below the music in regular verse form. The music has been written to fit the first stanza, and the remainder of the complete text, when sung, is forced into the pattern established for the first stanza.

While there will not be exact agreement of rhythm and stress between the remaining stanzas and music, strophic settings as shown in this composition are often found and they do often present added problems. From the following musical example, we can see more detail of some problems inevitably to be faced when we perform strophic settings.

A reading of the portions of verses one and two in the above example shows them to have the same metric pattern. But if we probe further we notice that, while the accents occur in the same metric sequence in both verses, the relative importance of the words appropriate to the accents is not at all the same. For example, look at "that's" and "chaste" on the third note. Obviously, "chaste" is of more importance in stanza two than is "that's" in stanza one. Observe the text set to the last six notes of the example; "true respects" appears to be in proper relationship to the music, but, in stanza two, "sets" is given only one-half beat while "the" is given three times that length. To point out these problems is not to fault Byrd in particular, for strophic settings appear in every age. But the above example does bring to mind again the fact that strophic music ordinarily sets the first verse more correctly than it sets the remainder of the text. Before we choose strophic settings of music to perform, we would be well advised to check all stanzas and their relationship to the music.

Byrd often placed the main emphasis in one of the upper voices, usually the top voice, and gave the other voice parts an accompanying role. Although he was one of the first to write madrigals in England, his style is perhaps among the most advanced. The madrigal was frequently polyphonic; when set polyphonically, the vocal lines form a unified whole, but they also are more or less independent of one another. This results generally in more complicated rhythm and in greater difficulty in making the text clearly understood. Because of these characteristics, it is of particular importance to have strong and matched voices sing each part.

A second example is "Weep, O mine eyes" by John Bennet and is taken from *Madrigalis to Foure Voyces*, 1599.

> Weep, O mine eyes, and cease not,
> These your springtides, alas, methinks, increase not.
> O when, O when begin you
> To swell so high that I may drown me in you?

The poet here has given expression to great unhappiness; all four lines clearly show deep dismal feelings. The music moves mostly in long notes; the tonality is generally in minor; and there is use of the Picardy third.

Perhaps the most important line of the poem is the first, for the whole story seems to be contained in that first line. The remaining three lines simply reinforce what is essentially contained in the first line. The most important single word appears to be the first, "weep," for the essence of the stanza is found there. The composer could hardly ignore this emphasis inherent in the poem; he repeats that first line more often than any other; and he gives special attention to that first word.

Weep, O Mine Eyes

John Bennet

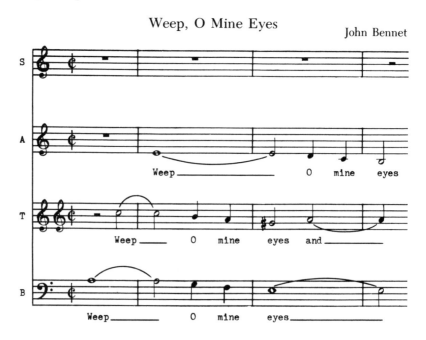

The setting for line two is not at all unusual. The musical devices used are the ones that one would expect to hear, and this gives the text a compatible and normal setting.

Line three is given some special attention. "O when" is sung in whole notes in the tenor and bass parts, and there is a long slow melisma in the soprano and alto parts. All of line three is then repeated, and line four follows, set in a manner which expresses agitation. The closing measures repeat the final phrase of the text, "that I may drown me in you," which is set in a deliberate fashion, and the music setting the last two lines of poetry is repeated.

The repeating of an entire section of a madrigal without change is not uncommon. But this was not the only device used to extend the four- and six-line lyrics into acceptable length. It was common also to incorporate a fugal treatment, giving the tune and the poem to each of the various voices, while the other voices added emphasis and embellishment where needed.

In connection with this matter of repetition, the question arises whether composers followed the poem as actually written by the author. And in many instances, this question cannot adequately be resolved, for only a small number of these texts can be found in sources other than where they are set to music. But such sources as do exist appear to reveal that most composers were reluctant to make substantial changes in the poems. Only occasionally were alterations made.

Repetition, which cannot actually be called a misrepresentation of the poet's text, is used frequently and effectively. It has been shown that repetition is a part of Thomas Campion's musical and literary style. Those literary transcriptions of his poetry which omit repetitions fail to include the device which makes them most effective. The same observation could be made of the works of other poets, for repetition is one of the most important means of achieving unity. And its use in the English madrigal is no exception.

Rhythmic Freedom

The Elizabethan lyric which has the same rhythmic and metric patterns throughout is quite rare. The number of feet in the lines of a verse usually vary greatly, and the rhythm within each unit also changes frequently under usual circumstances. The best poets had such a refined sense of the difference between meter and rhythm that they gained both unity and variety without compromising greatly. "Adieu, sweet Amaryllis" from John Wilbye's first set of madrigals can serve as an example of this freedom from rhythmic monotony.

Ădiéu, sẅeet Ámăryllĭs,
Fŏr sińce tŏ párt yŏur wĭll ĭs,
Ŏ héavy tíding,
Heře iś fŏr mé nŏ bíding.
Yet ońce agaiń, ěre thát Ĭ párt wĭth yóu,
Ámăryllĭs, sẅéet, ădiéu.

Note the differences in each line. Even with the changes, the accents occur with regularity and the rhyming follows a definite scheme. As a result, we find clear organization with variety.

Formal Freedom

The lyric is variable in form, and it is usually short. It may have just four lines, but it may also consist of several verses. The six-line stanza is the most common, and to include a refrain is not uncommon. But, to include a refrain is clearly an accomodation of the poet to the musician. The number of stanzas and the use of a refrain also varies from one poem to another, and, of course, the music follows the form of the poetry. Occasionally there seem to be discrepancies; for example, the composer may appear to repeat a line or section which may not have been repeated by the poet. But there is evidence to show that poets anticipated and even wrote out repetitions to be used in the settings of their works. There also are instances where the composer took unwarranted liberties by adding and, perhaps altering, words or phrases of the text. One of the composers who most often changed the text was Thomas Morley, a composer whom we might least suspect.

The Music

We can best understand these madrigals if we realize that the music has as its purpose to dramatize and amplify the poetry. Without the text, the music loses much of its reason for being. Without the music, the text loses the medium in which it is best expressed.

Since the music and text are so closely related, musical freedom is possible only when the poem is free, for the poetry exercises certain restrictions upon the music.

- The music should best follow the rhythm of the text.
- Musical pitch should aid in our understanding of verbal inflections.
- Cadences in the text and music should coincide.
- The form of the music should be compatible with that of the text.
- The setting will be best when the focal points of the music and text coincide.

Freedom of musical rhythm is interpreted to mean freedom from meter rather than freedom from all restrictions. As was mentioned previously, metric patterns vary considerably from line to line and sometimes even within a line. The same fluid characteristic is desirable in the music, and this point often gives the music a character different from the more usual strict adherence to the barline. Much vocal music is set so that the text is forced into a strict metrical scheme where it must remain no matter to what extent the poetic rhythm is destroyed. This is not generally the situation with the English madrigal, for here music and poetry shared the same inflections and stresses. The composers were not trying to free themselves from the "tyranny of the barline," for such a strict concept had not yet developed. To them, the text to be used in one of these compositions was a much greater disciplining factor than were the texts they had chosen for their sacred compositions.

Freedom of sonority is quite an appropriate point, for sonorities as found in the English madrigal are often a result rather than the planned objective of composition. In general, the cadence was the planned harmonic device, and the cadence was so constructed as to coincide with the cadence in the text. The mood of the composition was often determined by the emotion contained in the text, and this element was complemented musically by the use of a major or minor mode, or sometimes by the use of ecclesiastical modes. Strict tonality as we know it was not yet common.

We can readily find rules to be followed in the church music of this time, but composers largely disregarded these rules in their secular compositions. They could not, of course, escape recognizing the generally accepted idiom of their time, even though they did often desire more freedom to experiment. So, we should look upon the madrigal as a type of vocal chamber music, rather than as a definite musical form. Both text and music remain essentially fluid, and this very characteristic bears directly upon the question: Should a conductor be used to conduct madrigals in a normal concert setting? Since we should attempt to move past usual metronomic markings toward more detailed representation of the actual inflections of text and music, it is easy to see that the usual function of a conductor is less in demand here than in much larger works. Performance will be best if the singers are arranged informally, perhaps around a table, and if there is little or no appearance of conducting. But, if your choir requires a conductor in order to perform this music adequately, the recommendation is that you conduct during the performance rather than omit this music entirely from the experience of your performers. As always, a few moments of rehearsal time taken to make your singers aware of this point will be well spent, for their understanding of what is actually desired will be enhanced. That greater understanding will be reflected in your performances.

8

The Relationship
of the Conductor
to the Music Performed

Since it is the conductor himself who prepares the musical score, rehearses, and conducts concerts, the training of the conductor is an important topic for us to consider. There are areas common to the training of all conductors, but there are also studies and experiences that are of particular importance to the conductor of choral music. Those who have conducted singers, bands, and orchestras know that these performers rehearse differently, and every active choral conductor will at some time be called upon to conduct music that also requires instruments. These are important topics for discussion, and the assumption will be made here that the reader has had some experience in these matters.

We shall be concerned with elements that will aid in proper preparation of the music, rather than with basic conducting patterns and techniques. But the point of view advocated is that we should not only be concerned with the initial training of the beginning choral conductor. We should give equal attention to continued study and experience throughout our career. Four areas requiring special attention are discussed on the following pages.

1. Understanding Voice Production

It is important that the choral conductor have a comprehensive understanding of voice production. There has been some tendency to minimize this area of preparation, and, as a result, some conductors may be less able to draw the full sound potential from their singers. Since our performing ensembles always include singers and often singers with limited voice training, the building of vocal sound is one of the most fundamental areas of initial training. It is equally important for us to have some advanced experience in singing, for, as is well known, if we do not use our own voice we may to some degree be out of touch with what our singers experience.

There are books written that discuss vocal technique, and it is necessary for us to be acquainted with standard sources. However, it is recommended that young singers and singers with little or no voice training study with a teacher. Individual attention is important, and the experienced teacher can more easily judge when to recommend exposure to different ideas and methods of voice production.

2. Understanding Repertoire and Conducting Technique

It is important to receive the best musical education available. Not only should one's education include training in analysis, music history, ear training, and other subject matter normally included in the music curriculum, but special attention should be given to repertoire and conducting technique. Performers will be most secure when there is clear and accurate direction. And this training and background will not only aid in communication during rehearsal and performance, but it will also help the conductor in his preparation of the score before rehearsals begin. Knowledge of subjects such as those discussed in Chapter 6 will aid in our choosing of more authentic editions and in the making of decisions about a particular performance. But this study should be in addition to more usual instruction. Also, it is important for us to hear many different choirs perform. If the young conductor hears varied choral performance and also has the advantage of having been exposed to the latest advances in the field, it will be possible for that person to develop a breadth of understanding more quickly than if he had only known one choral experience.

3. Understanding People

The choral conductor will be most successful if he is interested in people and not only in music. Perhaps we cannot change a person's basic interest, but we can acquire information, and we may describe this particular information as being in the fields of group dynamics, leadership, and human behavior. In actual practice, we will often draw upon information we have acquired in any or all of these areas. There may even be other fields that will provide helpful information in specific instances. In any event, we would be well advised not to ignore the fact that we are working with people. If a feeling of trust can be developed, our singers will have a greater sense of well-being, and it is well known that singers will actually perform better when this state of mind is present. This should not be an attempt to "use" people, but our attitude should be to have a genuine interest in our performers.

A word of caution is in order; study and associations such as are being advocated here are no substitute for musical and/or vocal training. Each is a part of the whole process of education, and these matters should complement one another. But no one area should be considered as a substitute for any other.

4. Understanding Non-Musical Subjects

A study of non-musical subjects is important to the choral musician for several reasons. A knowledge of languages and diction is of central importance to any performer of vocal music. Information about the literature and art of a country or period can also be quite helpful, and information about the physical characteristics of sound can help to utilize principles of acoustics in conducting rehearsals and performances. Even selected studies in such diverse fields as speech and physical education may be useful; studies in the field of speech can aid diction, and selective study in physical education can give information that will assist in understanding the function of one's body while singing.

While no single program of training can guarantee our bringing out the best in every student and making all equally successful, it is possible to look at successful persons and begin to determine the reasons for their success. It can be defeating to imitate any one performer or conductor, but information acquired by more comprehensive observation of those who have been successful cannot be consumed in any other way. No one should expect to accumulate all this information in a few short years; what we are discussing here takes a lifetime of work and study to acquire.

BASIC MUSICAL ELEMENTS AND THE PERFORMER

Mastering the elements of music and their execution is another fundamental area of study that we should undertake before we begin rehearsals. Conductor and performers alike should have already acquired a basic grasp of most usual musical elements to be found in the music they are about to work with. But there is always the possibility of profiting from a review of topics that were once studied in detail but have not received our close attention for some time. Of course, there may be special subject areas that were never before explored fully. The following topics have been chosen because they are applicable to most, if not all, music in the performance repertoire. The topics are not listed in any order of importance.

The Importance of Melody

Since melody is what most people in our audience will remember after our concert has ended, it is one of the most inportant musical elements in our performance. It should be obvious that we need to clearly identify melody wherever it may occur, and it will be of further help if we look within the melodic line and identify its many facets. The following points are valid when we are studying a musical score in preparation for performance.

- Determine where the melody is to be found. Usually, the melody will be in the upper part, but sometimes this will not be the case. Conductor and singers alike need to be well aware of the melody regardless of its position.

- Examine the melody to determine if it contains long or short phrases. Closely associated with this point is the use of breath. If the phrases are unusually long, singers will need to know how to properly sustain the melodic line.

- Determine if there are chord patterns, sequences, and/or difficult intervals. Chord patterns and sequences will aid the singers in mastering the music and should be called to their attention. Difficult intervals will take more rehearsal time to master, and the conductor should allow extra time from the very first reading.

- Observe the range and tessitura of the melody. It is necessary for the music to be well within the vocal range of the singers if they are to project a full, mature sound. That point is of special importance when we are working with the melodic line.

- To what point does the melody build? A melodic line rises to a particular point and then turns downward. If the placement of the point to which the melody builds is clear to the conductor, the performers can rehearse correctly from the beginning.

- Look for patterns in the melody that will be useful in learning the composition. To some extent this includes chord patterns and sequences as listed above, but there may be other melodic patterns as well.

- Determine if the melody is in major, minor, or another feeling. Just as the choice of a key is important to a composer, determining the character of the melodic line is of equal importance to a performer.

The Vertical Aspect of Music

In choral singing, the voice usually participates harmonically, and each part interacts vertically. An important part of the conductor's preparation is to examine the harmonic flow of the composition. The conductor needs to recognize and call attention to the function of key chords, and it is possible to develop a facility for making such observations. The use of chord progressions, doubling, leading tones, et cetera, are among those techniques that should be examined, and the following points are among those that should be considered.

- Determine if the harmonic style points toward a particular period in music history. Since compositions of different periods conform to different styles of sound, a recognition of this point will give the conductor and singers alike a good start in knowing what characteristic sound to work toward.

- Determine if the composition is harmonic in structure, or if there are unison and/or polyphonic sections. The structure has a definite influence upon how the composition will best be rehearsed.

- Observe whether the chord progressions are natural. Chord progressions that are natural will require less rehearsal time than will a composition in which there are several awkward spots. Recognize this point before rehearsals begin and time will be saved.

- Examine modulations, if any, and determine how they are accomplished. Modulations frequently are points at which special care should be exercised, and previous study will tend to eliminate potential problems.

- If composed during the twentieth century, determine if the work is traditional, twelve-tone, or of another orientation. Since there have been many different avenues explored in the field of composition during this century, it is essential to give careful attention to the technique(s) used by the composer.

- Determine the importance and function of dissonance. Dissonance of some type is present in any period in music history, and its use has varied greatly. Attention to non-chord tones and other devices will aid in the process of mastering the harmonic techniques to be found in the music.

Rhythm: Physical Response and Intellectual Understanding

Mastering the rhythmic notation of a composition is one of the most important and difficult tasks, for this step involves the proper physical response plus an intellectual understanding. One basic step is to understand that eighth notes do not necessarily mean that they are to be performed quickly; all an eighth note indicates, for example, is that it is to be performed one-half the length of time of a quarter note. Notation is grouped so as to comprise a pulse, and it is necessary that choruses be able to maintain a steady pulse at a variety of tempi. The following are among the points to be given special attention in this area.

- Determine if there is one rhythmic pattern, or a group of patterns, that is central to the composition. Since rhythm is the basic element in music, it is most important to identify specifically the pattern or element that will be central to maintaining the rhythmic flow of the music.
- Associate rhythm with tempo. Complex rhythmic figures at a fast tempo are more difficult to master than the same rhythmic figures at a slower tempo, and the approach should be different.
- Check rhythmic problems that appear, particularly at meter changes. When a singer establishes a physical reaction to a given meter, it may be difficult to make the necessary changes quickly; previous recognition by the conductor will aid greatly in making such changes successfully.
- Determine as quickly as possible those portions of the composition where scanning can be used to aid in achieving rhythmic clarity. (See Chaper 1, criterion number 7, for further information about the use of scanning.)
- Associate musical rhythm with textual rhythm. If the composer has set the text well, the rhythm inherent in text and music will coincide. (See Chapter 7 for further information about this point.)

Dynamics: Composer and Editorial Markings

Dynamic markings require different responses in different compositions. A crescendo in a Romantic composition is to be interpreted differently than the same marking in a composition of the Classic period. Areas of special attention include the following.

- Determine the musical period in which the composition was created. Dynamic markings used in one period may not mean the same thing in music of another period, or it may be appropriate to use a wider range of dynamics in the music of one period than in the music of another time.

- Separate editorial markings from instructions given by the composer. Early music has too often been marked up by editors, and frequently these added markings do not add to authentic information. (See Chapter 6 for further information on this subject.)
- Determine precisely at what point in the music the dynamic change is to be at its greatest intensity. Most dynamic changes move gradually from soft to full or full to soft, and that movement at some point arrives at the new level. An important point is to determine exactly where that new level arrives.

Phrasing: Music and Text

This topic touches upon music, text, and use of the breath; the importance of the proper coordination of these areas can not be overemphasized. Considerations should include the following.

- Determine if the phrases in the music and text coincide. If the composer has set the text well, the phrase structure in the music and text will be compatible. Instances where they do not coincide present unnecessary problems to which there are no real and totally valid answers. (See Chapter 7 for further information.)
- Sing the music yourself to determine if your singers will be able to perform the phrases properly as written. Phrases that are too long for your singers to sing in one breath will give added problems, and the conductor should know the music well enough to make this determination before passing the music out for rehearsal.
- Prepare your singers to stagger their breathing if the phrases as written in the music are too long for them to sing in one breath. This is a technique that choral singers often use; it is not without some problem, but staggered breathing is a way to compensate for phrase problems that our singers encounter.
- Identify the points where each phrase and section of the composition focus. Just as dynamics, melody, and other elements have a point of focus, so do the phrases of the composition. Identifying these points and working with them in rehearsal will ultimately give your performance a greater degree of musicality.

- Consider the overall sweep of the composition and the place of each phrase in that total work. This is the observation of the whole; just as it is important to give special attention to each phrase, it is equally necessary to give your attention ultimately to the overall relationship of those parts within the total composition.

Accents: Actual and Implied

In this brief discussion, accents will be understood to encompass all instantaneous changes in volume. Accents are inherent in the meter of the composition, but there also may be instances where special emphasis is called for by the composer. Both types add interest to the music, and you should pay special attention to the following.

- Examine the music and text to observe if the accents coincide. Metric accents have been discussed previously under the topic of *Rhythm* and in Chapter 7, but there are accents that the composer has included for special effect. These instances also need to receive our special attention, for their proper execution can add interest to a performance.
- Give special attention to examples of text painting, if any. While this kind of accent will usually be more subtle, attention given to this technique of setting a text, when it does occur, will help to highlight the musicality of the performance. One simple example of the use of text painting is to have the music ascend quickly at the mention of a word such as "heaven."
- Look for changes in meter and the accompanying accent patterns. Changes in meter often are points that show some of the most radical changes in a composition, and changes in accents accompany meter changes. A simple recognition of this point will serve as a guide to further bring out the music.
- Look for any instances of unusual accents and determine the extent of any special accents called for in the music.

The Importance of a Proper Tempo

An obvious factor in the performance of any music is proper tempo, for finding a proper tempo is fundamental to achieving a secure performance. A tempo that is too fast or too slow can cause problems with breath, phrasing, and many other related areas. But the metronomic markings in a score, if any, should not always be taken strictly. Metronomic markings are to be taken seriously, but they also serve as a point of departure. Factors to be taken into consideration include the following.

- Observe tempo directions in the musical score. These may include metronomic markings and/or such terms as *andante*, *allegro*, et cetera. These form the most basic elements in your decision-making process, but there are also other factors.

- Consider the number of singers and their capability for sustaining a vocal line. A slightly slower tempo may be appropriate when performing a given composition with a large choir, and a slightly brighter tempo may be called for when performing the same music with a smaller choir. Ultimately, singers and conductor all will "feel" a particular tempo to be "right."

- Consider the physical characteristics of the hall in which the music will be performed. Some halls are "alive" and others are "dry." The type of hall does make a difference, and you are encouraged to always take this factor into consideration.

- Finally, put it all together. Interpret known musical, physical, and vocal information to determine if your own performance tempo will be exactly that indicated in the music, or if your tempo will differ slightly from that given in the score.

MONOPHONY, POLYPHONY AND HOMOPHONY

The choral conductor's work is quite different when preparing homophonic music than it is when preparing music of another texture. Most singers will be more acquainted with performance practices appropriate to homophonic music. But experienced choral singers, like experienced instrumental performers, will have had much experience in performing polyphonic music as well. There is, of course, a tradition of monophonic texture as represented chiefly in Gregorian chant.

1. Gregorian Chant

Gregorian chant is liturgical music of the Catholic church.[1] This music presents an entirely different set of circumstances and problems. Monophonic music considered more generally is any music sung in unison. Since all voices sing the same vocal line, there is no problem of blending

---

[1] *The Liber Usualis* (New York; Desclee Company, 1959).

with other voices as there is in other more complex scores. Unison music which is well set, chant in particular, allows our attention to be focused upon one vocal line, and this music at its best can achieve a union of music and text not found in more complex musical scores. When conducting this type of score, it may be best to use a type of conducting gesture incorporated in *chironomy*, a gesture which shows the shape of the melodic line rather than one emphasizing the metric structure.

Any arrangement of Gregorian chant which includes an accompaniment and/or more than one part is to be avoided. Other unison compositions which have accompanying instrumental parts, like "The Sally Gardens" as arranged by Benjamin Britten and discussed in Chapter 2, will have one or more instrumental parts that complement the vocal line. In performing such music, you may wish to ask your singers to sing in the same way they would if they were performing an art song. If the vocal tone produced is free and open, you can blend the sound into a unit without difficulty.

2. Homophonic Choral Music

Homophonic choral music is of two general types: (1) music in which there is a melodic line in one part and chords in the other parts, and (2) music in which all voices sing the same text and move simultaneously.

The melodic line in the first type ordinarily moves more quickly than the chords. The melody will be in short notes, and the chordal parts will be in longer note values. The chords sometimes will be repeated, and in different music they may imitate an instrumental accompaniment. The chords are almost always subordinate to the melodic line. The second type ordinarily presents no particular problems in performance, unless the inner parts are sung by less mature singers. In either type of homophonic music, the accompanying or chordal parts need to be sung as interestingly and with as much importance as is the melodic line.

3. Polyphonic Music

Polyphonic music is often associated with the earlier musical periods, but there are examples of its use in every period currently in the performance repertoire. In any polyphonic music, and to a degree in all music, the singer needs to be aware of the relationship of his voice to the whole of the composition. The lines of a polyphonic composition may be identical in each part, or the vocal lines may move alternately—i.e., one part moves while another has a long note or notes and then the reverse. The long notes should be sung as subordinate to the moving part. But, in such a situation, the breath and tone still need to be kept vital; particular care should be taken to insure that singers drop long notes in sufficient time to enter the next active musical line on time, strongly, and with clarity. One commonly used rule is to shorten the long note in order to make the next entrance clearly and with authority.

INTERPRETATION AND TECHNIQUE

Technical information is essential, for such information serves as the basis upon which interpretation is formed. But to expect that a simple understanding and execution of technical detail will provide sufficient basis for mature interpretation of music is not to understand fully the nature of the art. There is little doubt that, traditionally, too little emphasis has been placed upon the accumulation of facts concerning the music and performers, and the present study gives further support for the gathering of such factual information. But we all need to realize that the proper remedy for this situation is to also recognize the importance of what we call musicality. To argue in support of either technique or basic musicality to the exclusion of the other is to create a dilemma where there should be none. As has been said, the proper answer to any question you may have concerning the relationship of technique to musicality is to realize that we cannot properly ignore either aspect.

Aaron Copland delivered the commencement address at Brooklyn College, in June, 1975, and a brief excerpt from his remarks adds another dimension to the present discussion. While he was speaking more about the composer, the following remarks appear to apply to the conductor and performer as well.[2]

> The artist, I think, symbolizes the importance of the individual—only he or she can create the work that is created. Moreover, the artist is in a continuing state of self-discovery, because each new work is a new exploration in what one's creative mind is able to bring forth. The artist's life is a belief in the possibility of perfectability. Each time you finish a work and start a new one, that new one presents again a new challenge. . . . So the artist is, in a sense, a kind of gambler. He gambles on his own belief in himself. . . .

---

[2]From the *Newsletter of the Institute for Studies in American Music*, Rita H. Mead, Acting Editor, November 1975, Vol. V, No. 1.

Any one of us who succeeds in all these areas should have conquered average kinds of problems; he will have risen far above the average. He will continue to have problems, but the level of those problems will show that person to be among the most successful in the field of choral music.

PART THREE

WRITING

9

Composers of
American Choral Music:
Their Compositions and Practices

Part Three of this book is devoted to a discussion of topics pertinent to music writing; much information will concern actual rules and examples. But this chapter will deal as much with the development of choral music in the United States.

While articles have been written that discuss aspects of the development of choral music in this country, there has been no real effort to deal with the subject since the beginning of choral performance in this country. This chapter will be devoted to a discussion of the music and performance practices of outstanding composers of choral music in the United States.

INDIVIDUAL COMPOSERS WHO CONTRIBUTED
MOST TO THEIR TIME

William Billings (1746-1800)

Some of the most distinctive eighteenth century choral music in the United States was written by William Billings. "Chester" and "When Jesus Wept" are but two representative examples among many compositions that were widely distributed and that now receive numerous performances. "Chester" is set in four-part strophic hymn style, while "When Jesus Wept" is one of a series of fuguing tunes. Fuguing tunes served as an important body of choral music. Many of their singers were not trained as well as are today's singers, and this music was within the grasp of most. The following example shows this most prominent fuguing tune.[1]

When Jesus Wept

William Billings

Billings' choral music can be described as having folk-like melodies; its harmony contains many fifths and octaves and occasional unusual dissonant treatment; its form is often rudimentary; and its rhythm often resembles dance patterns. Billings was not primarily interested in having his music performed by trained musicians. He was quite interested in composing music that would aid the common man in learning more about music by cultivating his interest in the art of singing.

---

[1]Marrocco, W. Thomas and Gleason, Harold (eds.), *Music In America* (N.Y.: W.W. Norton & Company, Inc., 1964), p. 111.

The assignment of singers to different voice parts is an important consideration for the choral conductor before he performs Billings' music. Billings' comments not only give his own ideas, but his comments also attempt to refute those ideas of his contemporaries that he believed to be in error.

During the last part of the eighteenth century, several American-born composers appeared in New England, especially around Boston, and their vocal compositions, primarily hymns, psalm tunes, and anthems, comprised much of the vocal music that was available to singers in the United States at that time. Along with Billings, there were other composers such as Francis Hopkinson, Daniel Read, and Samuel Holyoke. But the music of William Billings is considered to be more important than any other of those American-born composers. He not only composed much music, but his six published books on music composition also included many comments on musical practices of his time. Billings' music and writing, then, serve as primary source material for studying the composition and performance of early choral music in this country. The following points summarize the more important of Billings' ideas and practices:

- His music is for a four-part mixed chorus, but the number of voice parts can be increased by (1) having the treble and tenor parts sung by a full combination of men's and women's voices, (2) making use of *divisi* parts in the upper two voice parts, and (3) making use of the *ground bass* as an additional part, possibly also having that part doubled by an instrument. Billings wished at least half of his singers to be basses in order to have what he considered to be a proper balance.

- The four-syllable *fasola* system of solmization was used when learning this music. The use of syllables was also thought to be important for, when syllables were used, the sacred text was not compromised or profaned during the learning process.

- Tempos were thought of as basically one quarter note per second, with the shape of the time signature indicating the specific tempo. The basic tempo was modified at points where the composer included such terms as *Allegro* or *Slow*.

- In choosing a particular psalm tune, the director was well advised to consider if the tonality of the tune suited the meaning of the psalm text, i.e., one would choose a tune in minor for a prayer and a tune in major for a "Psalm of Praise and Thanksgiving."

- A pitch pipe was used for giving the pitch of a composition, and the pitch as written was changed if the director found the written pitch not suited to his particular singers.
- Billings used the "Mark of Distinction," a type of accent; but he was opposed to using the *fermata*.
- The custom of "lining out the psalm" was then in use, and this practice caused Billings considerable annoyance.
- Singers were allowed three types of ornamentation of the melody: (1) the "Single-Trill," the mordent; (2) the "Double-Trill," a type of turn; and (3) the "Grace of Transition," a *portamento* effect.

While Billings and his contemporaries were only modestly trained in music, they and their compositions exerted an important influence on musical life in this country. After them, more highly trained musicians from Europe came to take positions in the United States. And it was primarily those European-trained musicians who kept choral activity active here until late in the nineteenth century. There were numerous choral societies, and the *Saenger-Fests*, held in Baltimore, Philadelphia and New York, were large undertakings that have no equal today. But the music chosen for performance came primarily from Europe.

Horatio Parker (1863-1919)

Parker stood quite near the top of the Boston group, many of whom received much of their training in Germany. Parker, himself, studied with George Chadwick and later spent a period of time studying in Europe. After three years abroad, he settled in New York City as a church organist and faculty member of the National Conservatory. He later became Professor of Music at Yale University, and was quite active as a choral conductor. He composed nearly three dozen choral works, including oratorios, cantatas and octavo compositions. But one of his works was performed both in the United States and in Europe, and *Hora Novissima* came to be known as his acknowledged masterpiece.

Various writers have compared parts of *Hora Novissima* to the music of Bach, Palestrina, and other master composers. But the principal point is simply this; the work was composed in this country, and it is an early example of choral music that equalled the music being composed during the same time period by many acknowledged musicians in Europe.

Parker's cantata did help to set a standard for American choral music, but it did not serve as a work that could be recognized as strictly American.

It would be for later American composers to give us music unique to this country.

Harry Burleigh (1866-1949)

Burleigh was one of the earlier black composers to make a lasting contribution to the field of choral music. He was a baritone and he first made a career of singing, but he left us some fifty choral compositions.

Burleigh obtained a scholarship to the National Conservatory of Music in New York City, where he studied composition with Antonin Dvorak. It was Dvorak who most encouraged Burleigh in his composition, for it was Dvorak's view that American composers should write music that could be identified as particular to this country. His view was that too many American composers were imitating their European counterparts. Certainly, Burleigh's original compositions and arrangements of spirituals did much to bring such music to the attention of audiences everywhere. His music shows nationalistic influences, and his own influence has been an important help to other black composers who followed him. In 1900, Burleigh became a music editor for Ricordi and Company, and this association led to the publishing of his choral compositions and arrangements. His music always emphasizes the melodic line, but he also has made use of some dissonance to add color.

Charles Ives (1874-1954)

Ives was one of the most unique composers in the history of American music. His *Sixty-Seventh Psalm* has been discussed in Chapters 2 and 5, and it must be considered to be his most often performed choral composition. But there is other music which also shows the uniqueness of Ives's contribution. Your attention is called, in particular, to *Psalm 90* and the three *Harvest Home Chorales*. Of these compositions, *Psalm 90* has been chosen for discussion here.

The form of *Psalm 90* can be viewed as generally a two-part form. Ives's subtitle of "Declamations and Prayer" suggests a division of verses one through thirteen as the "Declamations" and verses fourteen through seventeen as the "Prayer."

The opening organ introduction used seven chords in unmeasured rhythm, and five of the chord structures were called: (1) The Eternities; (2) Creation; (3) God's Wrath Against Sin; (4) Prayer and Humility; and (5) Rejoicing in Beauty and Work. Each of these chords, like the entire composition, is set to a low C pedal in the organ. Above this pedal are ninth, eleventh, and thirteenth chords. Ives used such techniques as bitonal chords, tone clusters, imative and free counterpoint, and large skips, especially in the outer voices. Unison singing is also frequent with sudden movement to thick chordal structures of from eight to twenty-two different voice parts. The principle of common tones between chords is maintained at times, but wherever Ives wished to highlight a single word, he moved almost any interval to achieve the desired effect. Consequently, seconds, fourths, sevenths, and other intervals are often required of the singers. The most traditional part writing occurs in the last portion of the composition, and one particularly striking and difficult passage is shown in the following example.

TWENTIETH-CENTURY COMPOSERS
WHO CAME TO THE UNITED STATES

Ernest Bloch (1880-1959)

Bloch was born in Switzerland. He lived in the United States from 1916 to 1930, and he again lived here after 1939. His *Sacred Service* (*Avodath Hakodesh*, 1934), for baritone soloist, chorus and orchestra, uses as its text the Jewish Sabbath Morning Service. And it is often called the most important of Bloch's Jewish works. The style of the *Sacred Service* is not particularly complicated, in contrast to the more complex and less traditional instrumental compositions, But it is not actually unique for a composer to follow a more traditional design in his choral compositions.

Sacred Service contains the traditional five parts, with each part being further subdivided; the first and third parts have instrumental preludes for orchestra or organ. The effect of the music is cumulative; the chanting of the soloist and the singing of the choir all move toward the last section. In that last section "the soloist (as the Cantor) intones in a quasi-speaking voice a long and moving prayer for the establishment of God's kingdom on earth, and for the fellowship of all men."[2]

Igor Stravinsky (1882-1971)

Stravinsky is an important composer of choral music even though we may view his orchestral compositions as his most significant repertoire. His *Pater Noster* and *Ave Maria* are included in Chapter 2, and they are most often listed among his neo-classic compositions. But most of his choral compositions are in large forms.

Stravinsky's early interest in Romanticism is, perhaps, best shown in the *Lament on the Death of Rimsky-Korsakov* (1908) for chorus and orchestra. The seldom performed *King of the Stars* (1911), for male chorus and orchestra, and *Saucers* (1914-17), four Russian songs for female voices, are also from this same early period. In general, his early choral works show the influence of Russian folk music.

Les Noces (*The Wedding*, 1923) requires four soloists, chorus, and a percussion ensemble that includes four pianos; the text concerns Russian wedding customs. Much of Stravinsky's music up to this time had been nationally motivated, but *Les Noces* was different in that it did not show a particular Russian stamp. While the work is quite Russian in subject matter, it does move Stravinsky closer to the mainstream of European music that he would later join.

---

[2]Jacobs, Arthur (ed.), *Choral Music: A Symposium* (Baltimore: Penguin Books, 1963), p. 357.

While *Pater Noster* and *Ave Maria* are included among Stravinsky's neo-classic compositions, several large works are also properly included here. The are (1) the opera-oratorio *Oedipus Rex* (1927-28); (2) the *Symphony of Psalms* (1930), for chorus and orchestra; and (3) the *Mass* (1951), for two oboes, English horn, two bassoons, two trumpets, three tombones, men's voices, and children's voices.

The *Symphony of Psalms* was Stravinsky's first large religious composition, and he makes stylistic concessions to the religious character of the text. The choral parts are often slow and stately, and rapid movement is emphasized in the orchestra. It would be difficult to exaggerate too greatly the importance of this work. To employ a large chorus was the only practical means at Stravinsky's disposal, for the ritual itself gives wide scope for employing the choir's expressive resources. The results are impressive, and this work stands as a large-scale religious composition of the twentieth century where the effort involved in performance preparation is copiously rewarded at the actual performance.

His tendency toward orchestral restraint is shown particularly in the *Cantata* (1952) for soprano, tenor, and female chorus. *Cantata* is based upon anonymous fifteenth- and sixteenth-century English texts, accompanied by flutes, oboes, English horn, and cello. Stravinsky's more recent twelve-tone compositions include: (1) *Canticum Sacrum* (*Sacred Canticle*; 1955) and (2) *Threni, id est Lamentationes Jeremiae prophetae* (*Lamentations of Jeremiah*; 1957-58).

His music is expected to remain in the repertoire as long as any composed during the twentieth century. Most of Stravinsky's compositions require mature performers; particular care should be taken before any choral conductor places one or more of these compositions in the performance repertoire of his choir.

Paul Hindemith (1895-1963)

Hindemith made a significant contribution to the field of choral music. His *Six Chansons* are included in the music discussed in Chapter 2, and his interest in *Gebrauchsmusik* (music for use) is felt in choral music just as it is felt in other fields. *Frau Musica* (*In Praise of Music*; 1928) perhaps best shows his interest in choral *Gebrauchsmusik*. It sets a text by Martin Luther; it is a small four-movement cantata; and the instruments include strings, with flute and other instruments ad libitum.

In the first part of *Frau Musica*, everyone, including the audience, sings a melody in transposed Dorian mode. And in the closing chorus, the full choir and audience sings a song of praise. This is relatively simple music and it represents a significant departure from the more usual emphasis on virtuoso performers in favor of music that is within the performance capability of many choirs. A revised edition, 1945, provides an English translation of the Luther text.

During the years that he was Professor of Composition at Yale University, Hindemith made a real effort to come to terms with American music. Perhaps his most known composition of this time is *When Lilacs Last in the Dooryard Bloom'd* (1946), with text by Walt Whitman.

Lukas Foss (1922-   )

Foss came to this country after having been born in Germany. His secular cantata, *The Prairie*, with text taken from a poem by Carl Sandburg, is for four-part choir, four soloists, and orchestra. It is divided into seven different portions which use various performance combinations. This cantata is about equally divided between chordal and contrapuntal writing; there are ostinato figures in the bass; there are several modulations; and it is basically tonal.

A Parable of Death (1952) is based on verses by Rainer Maria Rilke and is for narrator, tenor soloist, chorus, and orchestra. Foss's gift for lyricism is particularly evident in this work.

THOSE COMPOSERS WHO WERE NATIVE AMERICANS

Howard Hanson (1896-   )

Hanson is among the conservative neo-Romantic American composers. He has made a contribution to American music as a teacher, administrator, and conductor. But it is as a composer that he is best known. *Lament for Beowulf* (1925) is among his better known choral compositions. The work is set for four-part choir and orchestra, and the choral parts are often in chordal style, occasionally alternating with imitative parts. There are several meters, and the orchestra is often sustained, giving the mood of somberness.

Virgil Thomson (1896-   )

Thomson shows his interest in early hymns in *Symphony on a Hymn Tune* (1928). His smaller works include *Three Antiphonal Psalms* (1924), for unaccompanied women's chorus, and *Missa Brevis* (1936), for women's chorus and percussion instruments. Some of Thomson's better choral writing is to be found in his operas, *Four Saints in Three Acts* and *The Mother of Us All*. But one of his later works is also one of his more ambitious. *Missa Pro Defunctis* was composed for and received its premier performance by the Crane Chorus of the State University of New York-Potsdam on May 14, 1960. It is an important work that deserves to be performed more.

Randall Thompson (1899-   )

Thompson composed quite successfully both in large and small forms. His *Frostiana* and *The Last Words of David* are included in Chapter 2, and *Alleluia* (1940) continues to be one of the most inspiring and often performed octavo compositions by an American composer. *Alleluia* is for unaccompanied chorus, it is a traditional composition, and it must be looked upon as a model among small, contemporary, American choral compositions.

Thompson's larger choral compositions are no less important. The mass is one of the oldest forms of vocal music still in the repertoire, and Thompson's *Mass of the Holy Spirit* (1955-56) is a well-known representative of the twentieth century. The music is essentially for four-part choir, but it does contain solo passages. Occasionally, it requires an eight-part chorus. It is well known that Thompson writes within the traditional tonal system, and the writing in this *Mass* is no exception. The keys of A major and a minor are predominant, with the Gloria being set in D major.

Thompson makes full use of a variety of textures and vocal styles "ranging from highly melismatic through antiphonal to involved polyphonic. . . . Fugues and canons occur in several movements, notably a three-voice canon in the "Christe eleison," a four-voice canon in the "Blessed Is He" (Benedictus), and a two-voice canon with two free contrapuntal parts in the "Lamb of God" (Agnus Dei)."[3]

The Peaceable Kingdom (1936) is for unaccompanied mixed chorus, and it is divided into eight choruses. The music is said to have been suggested by a painting of the same title by the early nineteenth-century American artist, Edward Hicks. Hicks was a Quaker minister.[4] The mood of this music varies from somber to jubilant; the text speaks of the reward for the righteous and the fate of the wicked; and Thompson includes chordal sections, imitative and antiphonal writing, melismas, and choral recitative. The text is taken from the Book of Isaiah.

The Testament of Freedom (1943) has a text selected from the writings of Thomas Jefferson. It is set for four-part men's chorus; it utilizes a stan-

---

[3]Ulrich, Homer, *A Survey of Choral Music* (N.Y.: *Harcourt* Brace Jovanovich, Inc., 1973), p. 188.
[4]Chase, Gilbert, *America's Music* (N.Y.: McGraw-Hill Book Co., 1966), p. 535.

dard orchestra; and the work is divided into four movements. The strong rhythmic accompaniment in the orchestra emphasizes the spirit expressed in the text, and unison writing predominates in the chorus. This music has been characterized as a kind of public music which possesses grandeur while still utilizing relatively simple structural means.

Aaron Copland (1900-   )

Copland is now generally considered to be the "Dean of American Composers," and one can hardly omit some mention of his work in the choral field. His *In the Beginning* (1947) is for unaccompanied chorus, and, while some of his choral writing may give the appearance of folk music, this composition does not fall into such a classification.

Perhaps it is in his operas that some of his most known choral writing appears. For example, "Stomp Your Feet," from *The Tender Land*, continues to be an attractive short composition for chorus. But Copland's craftsmanship may be shown most clearly in the *Canticle of Freedom*, a short composition for chorus and orchestra which dates from the mid-1950's.

William Schuman (1910-   )

Schuman, like Howard Hanson, has made a considerable contribution as a teacher and administrator. But he, too, made a significant contribution to the field of choral music. One need not look farther than to his *Cantata No. 2*, which won a Pulitzer Prize in 1942. Schuman was a practicing choral conductor at Sarah Lawrence College, and he has known choral music as a conductor as well as from the point of view of a composer.

Schuman may be termed an eclectic composer whose most lasting compositions are for orchestra. But his choral compositions do add significantly to the American choral heritage. From the period of his greatest involvement in choral music came *Choral Étude* (1937), for unaccompanied chorus; his setting of Whitman's *Pioneers!* (1937), for unaccompanied chorus in eight parts; and *This Is Our Time* (1940), for chorus and orchestra. His octavo choral compositions also include such works as *Prelude* and *Holiday Song*.

Perhaps Vincent Persichetti best stated the characteristics of Schuman's compositional style, when he wrote:

> Schuman does not use tonality for structural purposes. . . . He covers the wide gamut of scales bestowed upon Occidental civilization, and needs the elbow room afforded by the freedom of shifting modes, "twelve-tone" melodies if he chooses, but always a tonality. . . . Some of his harmony is misunderstood. The much mentioned polytonality in Schuman is not

polytonality but polyharmony. Triads of kindred tonalities joining to form one resonant five- or six-note chord result in a harmony enriched by overtones and belonging to one key. He is fond of these chords and can manipulate them by adjusting the dissonant relationship of the chord-members to acquire any texture he needs.[5]

Samuel Barber (1910-   )

Barber was a trained singer and he seems to have particular insight in writing for the human voice. While his operas and songs may be better known to the general public than are his choral compositions, he has contributed much significant choral music. *Sure on this Shining Night*, as included in Chapter 2, was originally an art song, and Barber himself set this lovely melody for chorus.

Barber's early choral works include *The Virgin Martyrs* (1935), for four-part women's chorus, and *Let Down the Bars, O Death* (1936), for four-part mixed chorus. It was with *A Stopwatch and an Ordnance Map* (1940), for men's chorus, timpani, and optional horns, trombones and tuba, that his music came to the general attention of choral musicians. But his later writing was to include his most significant compositions.

The *Prayers of Kierkegaard* (1953-54), for solo soprano, optional alto and tenor soloists, mixed chorus and orchestra, is set to a text based on the writings of Søren Kierkegaard, a nineteenth-century Danish philosopher. The work contains four connected but contrasting sections: (1) section one begins with a passage for unaccompanied men's voices in plainsong style and continues in mixed chordal and imitative style; (2) section two is a solo for the soprano; (3) section three is largely in chordal style, and the choir is divided into halves that occasionally sing antiphonally; and (4) section four is essentially for orchestra, with the choir entering only in the final twenty-six measures.[6]

Norman Dello Joio (1913-   )

Dello Joio has shown a gift for writing melody, and his study with Hindemith helped to shape his writing toward his neo-classical tendencies. His writing is sometimes lyrical and sometimes impressively large. Dello Joio, like so many composers in this country, has set writings of Whitman to music.

The Mystic Trumpeter (1943) is for soprano, tenor, and baritone soloists, chorus, and French horn or piano, and this composition called the attention of many musicians to Dello Joio's choral writing. The *Song of*

---

[5]Schreiber, Flora R. and Persichetti, Vincent, *William Schuman* (N.Y.: G. Schirmer, Inc.), 1954, p. 58.
[6]Ulrich, Homer, *A Survey of Choral Music*, p. 208.

Affirmation (1944) is a cantata for mixed chorus, narrator, soprano soloist, and orchestra, and *A Psalm of David* (1951) utilizes a four-part chorus with orchestral or piano accompaniment. This last work is divided into three connected parts, and a cantus firmus, used by Josquin des Prez several centuries before when he set the same text, plays an important part in Dello Joio's setting. The cantus firmus is an eight-note phrase with all but one tone on E and that one other note on F. The cantus firmus appears in each section, and it rises with various rhythmic figures to successively higher pitch levels on the seven degrees of the scale. The remaining voices (1) engage in imitations of the cantus firmus, (2) give chordal support, or (3) sing in counterpoint with the cantus firmus. The accompaniment includes impressive rhythmic figures and several short interludes.

Alan Hovhaness (1911-   )

Hovhaness' father was Armenian, and he developed quite an interest in the chants of the Armenian Church, as well as more generally in oriental music. Some of his music is predominantly oriental; he had visited India and other countries; and he learned oriental music firsthand by working with native musicians in those countries he visited.

His *Magnificat* (1959), for four soloists, mixed chorus, and orchestra, contains several striking moments. At times in this music there are sections where the performers repeat a rhythmic passage rapidly, but not together, and move from a *pianissimo* to an impressive *fortissimo* before returning to a *pianissimo*. Such dynamic contrast only enhances the mystical effect of the text.

The *Thirtieth Ode of Solomon* (1949) is a cantata for baritone soloist, mixed chorus, trumpet, trombone, and string orchestra. The interesting musical colors have made this composition a work of importance.

Vincent Persichetti (1915-   )

Persichetti has not been among the most conservative or most experimental composers of choral music. His *Te Deum* (1964) is set for four-part choir and standard orchestra, but the choir may be expanded to eight voices. This work contains a variety of dissonances, but it is primarily in chordal style. There are also sections in unison, imitation, and choral declamation. There are several changes of musical meter that appropriately and carefully set the different meters present in the text.

Daniel Pinkham (1923-   )

Pinkham is not essentially an experimental composer. He has been interested in making his music accessible, and his own activity as a performing musician has had an influence on his composition.

Pinkham has been organist at Kings's Chapel in Boston, as well as a pianist, harpsichordist and conductor, and the composition of choral music has been an important part of his creative activity. He employs homophonic texture for the most part, and his occasional use of imitation is primarily for contrast.

His choral music includes (1) *Easter Cantata*, for mixed chorus, brass, celesta, timpani, and percussion; (2) *An Emily Dickinson Mosaic*, a cantata for women's chorus and small orchestra; (3) *Festival Magnificat and Nunc Dimittis*, for mixed chorus, optional brass, and organ; (4) *Requiem* for alto and tenor soloists, mixed chorus, trumpets, horns, trombones, and contrabass; and (5) *Sinfonia Sacra (Christmas Cantata)* for mixed chorus and brass instruments.

His *Lamentations of Job* (1966) is for four-part choir, brass, percussion, and contrabass, and this composition contains both chordal and imitative writing. The setting of one or two voices above or against the others gives this composition an attractive variety of color, and there are many meter changes as suggested by the text.

Leonard Bernstein (1918-   )

Bernstein is not ordinarily looked to for his choral compositions, but his *Mass* (1971), composed for the opening of the Kennedy Center for the Performing Arts in Washington, D.C., must be considered a special composition. *Mass* is for chorus, soloists, orchestra, rock bands, and dancers. Even the audience is invited to participate. It is not choral in the traditional sense, but its total impact must be considered to be enormous. *Mass* has lyrical and dramatic moments, and the total work embraces quite a wide variety of musical styles. While *Mass* is a recent work, Bernstein also included choral writing in his several previous works for the musical stage.

10

Musical Practices
for the Choral Music Writer

Writing music includes the recognition of certain common practices, and this chapter is devoted to an exploration of such practices. Choral conductors and teachers, perhaps more than those persons who work with instrumental music, frequently find it advantageous to change music to better suit the particular chorus. For example, it may happen that those particular tenors are not able to sustain a required tessitura.

Every choral conductor has had training in music theory and there are many good books available that deal with this general subject matter. But a shorter discussion directed more particularly to teachers of choral music can also be quite useful. The discussion here, then, will be devoted to pointing out situations that will be important to those of us who work in the field of choral music.

The three basic elements of any music are melody, rhythm, and harmony. Melody is normally given in the printed score, and the most essential rhythmic characteristics also may be shown in the melody. But harmony is an element which often can be profitably revised. When we discuss harmony, we consider both the vertical structure (chords) and the horizontal succession of chords. In addition, it should be pointed out that this discussion will be concerned predominately with tonal music, i.e., music in which there is a definite tonal center.

Music in a Major Key

Every scale degree has a name, and the chord based upon that particular scale degree is called by the same name. The following examples show all scale degrees and the principal chords in major; the example is in the key of C major.

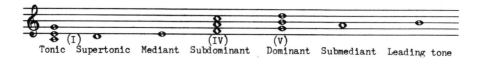

Tonic Supertonic Mediant Subdominant Dominant Submediant Leading tone

The *tonic* in the above example serves as the tonal center, and the first, fourth, and fifth steps serve as the bases for the principal chords. The second, third, sixth, and seventh steps serve as the bases for secondary chords. Principal chords are used more prominantly, but secondary chords also have an important place. The following example shows secondary chords, and it is also in the key of C major.

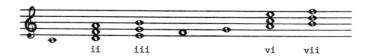

ii   iii   vi   vii

While each of the seven scale degrees serves as the basis for a particular chord, not all chords contain the same intervals. The following list shows the quality of the chords in any major key.

- The chord based on the 1st scale degree is *major*.
- The chord based on the 2nd scale degree is *minor*.
- The chord based on the 3rd scale degree is *minor*.
- The chord based on the 4th scale degree is *major*.
- The chord based on the 5th scale degree is *major*.
- The chord based on the 6th scale degree is *minor*.
- The chord based on the 7th scale degree is *diminished*.

An *augmented* chord contains two intervals of a major third; a *major* or a *minor* chord contains one major third and one minor third; and a *diminished* chord contains two minor thirds.

Music in a Minor Key

This music has a tonal center, just as does music in major. The terminology is the same as it is for music in major, and there are also principal and secondary tones. It is assumed that every choral musician already knows all major and minor keys. But the following examples in *a* minor will serve to show a representative example.

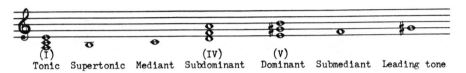

The *tonic* serves as the tonal center, and the first, fourth, and fifth steps again serve as the bases for the principal chords. Just as in any major key, the second, third, sixth, and seventh steps of any minor key form the bases for secondary chords.

Chords are as follows in the harmonic form of the minor.

- The chord based on the 1st scale degree is *minor*.
- The chord based on the 2nd scale degree is *diminished*.
- The chord based on the 3rd scale degree is *augmented*.
- The chord based on the 4th scale degree is *minor*.
- The chord based on the 5th scale degree is *major*.
- The chord based on the 6th scale degree is *major*.
- The chord based on the 7th scale degree is *diminished*.

Since I, IV and V are the primary chords, the succession of these three chords is of basic importance in achieving a satisfactory harmonic progression. It is generally agreed there are three usual progressions which involve primary triads; the progressions are as follows:

I – V – I
I – IV – I
I – IV – V – I

These progressions have been basic to music composition for centuries, and numerous examples can be found in music of the Baroque and later periods. In the simplest of terms, a I-IV-V-I progression may be as follows:

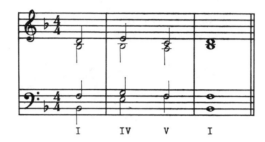

Compositions that use primary triads almost exclusively tend to sound quite positive, but too consistent use of primary chords may result in an entirely traditional sound that may tend to sound dull. Secondary chords are used to give variety and color to harmony that would not have enough color and interest without including them.

Each secondary chord is associated with a specific primary chord, and, when substituted for that primary chord, the secondary triad takes on a similar harmonic function. Closely associated primary and secondary chords are shown below; notice that each pair has two tones in common.

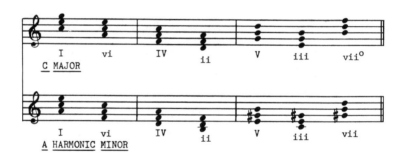

The usual distribution of voices is for the soprano to take the highest pitch, the alto to take the second highest pitch, the tenor to take the second lowest pitch, and the bass to take the lowest pitch. When these usual positions are not followed, two or more parts are said to be crossed.

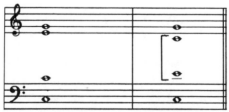

Normal distribution.   Alto and tenor voices are crossed.

Occasional crossing of voices is not always to be avoided, but it will ordinarily be best to maintain normal distribution until you become quite proficient in writing. Also, intervals between the soprano and alto, or the alto and tenor, should be no more than one octave. You should consider using an interval of more than one octave only between the tenor and bass, and, even then, only for particular instances. When a triad is in root position, the bass is to be doubled by one of the upper voices and the remaining two voices take the third and fifth of the chord.

Chords may be in *close* or *open* structure. The *close* structure is said to be used when the three upper voices are as close together as is possible. The *open* structure is used when there is a vacant triad tone between the soprano and alto, and between the alto and tenor voices.

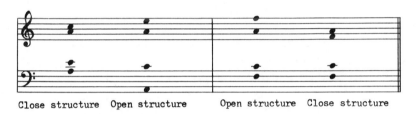

Close structure   Open structure   Open structure   Close structure

The following example from Brahms', *Ein deutsches Requiem* is primarily in *open* structure.

Ein deutsches Requiem

Voice Leading

When several chords occur in succession, as in an entire section or composition, it is best if each voice leads smoothly from one chord to the next. This will happen with relatively few leaps. When we look at the succession of chords from the horizontal view, it is important to see how voices relate to one another in terms of relative motion. There are four types of relative motion: (1) *similar*, (2) *parallel*, (3) *oblique*, and (4) *contrary*.

- *Similar* motion: the voices move in the same direction, either up or down, but not by the same interval.
- *Parallel* motion: the voices move in the same direction, either up or down, but also by the same interval.
- *Oblique* motion: one voice repeats the same pitch while the other voice moves either up or done.
- *Contrary* motion: the two voices move in opposite directions.

Similar motion   Parallel motion   Oblique motion   Contrary motion

It is important that no one type of relative motion be used to the exclusion of the other three types, for the music will tend to lack variety. Good voice-leading will be most possible when the majority of melodic intervals are seconds, and the leaps are largely either thirds or fourths. Small melodic intervals should predominate in each voice. The augmented second and the augmented fourth should be avoided as melodic intervals in choral music. These intervals are not easily sung, and to include one or both will only add problems.

When the same chord is written two or more times in succession as I — I, all tones of the triad will be common to both chords. In such an instance, it will simply be a matter of moving the voices within those same three tones. But where the progression involves chords whose roots are a fifth (or fourth) apart, there will be just one common tone. In chord successions where there is just one common tone, (1) the common tone may be retained in the same voice, and (2) all voices should move to the nearest chord tones which result in correct doubling and spacing.

Retain the common tone
in the same voice.

Move all voices to the nearest
chord tones for correct doubling
and spacing.

When we connect chords whose roots are a second apart, all upper voices normally move to the nearest chord tones in *contrary motion* to the bass. But when the bass moves up a second, one voice may move with the bass in parallel thirds or tenths, resulting in a doubled third in the second chord.

Upper voices move   One voice moves
contrary to the bass   parallel with the bass

The irregularity of doubling in the above example that shows a second voice moving parallel to the bass is most often used to avoid the augmented second which will otherwise occur when moving from V to VI in the harmonic minor.

When we use triads whose roots are a third apart, we normally should retain two common tones and move the remaining voice to the nearest chord tone. An alternative when the bass moves up a third is for one voice to move in parallel thirds or tenths with the bass, resulting in a doubled third in the second chord.

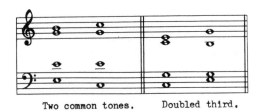

Two common tones.   Doubled third.

First and Second Inversions

All chords discussed previously have been shown in root position; the root has been in the lowest position. If the root is not the lowest tone, the chord is said to be *inverted*. There are three possible positions for a triad: (1) root position: the root is in the bass; (2) first inversion: the third is in the bass; and (3) second inversion: the fifth is in the bass. The figure 6 is used to identify a triad in first inversion, and $_4^6$ is used to identify a triad in second inversion.

Root position First inversion Second inversion

The use of inversions allows the bass line to move more smoothly, and this smooth movement contributes to greater melodic interest. Also, inversions give more variety.

Chords have a different character depending upon their position. Major and minor triads in root position give the most stable sonorities. Compositions almost always conclude with a chord in root position; triads in the first inversion are less stable. Since chords in first inversion are less stable, they tend to give a feeling of motion. Of course, forward motion is quite important to musical performance.

Chords in second inversion are even less stable than those that are in first inversion. Because chords in second inversion are also relatively less strong, they are to be used quite sparingly.

Practices to be followed when we work with chords in first inversion include the following.

- Double the soprano when a major or minor triad is in first inversion. When working with chords in this position, the doubled tone will vary according to which tone is in the soprano.
- When moving from a chord in first inversion to a chord in root position, (1) move the doubled tones to the nearest chord tones possible by *contrary, oblique,* or *similar* motion; and (2) move the remaining voice (or voices if that tone is doubled) to the chord tone that will complete the triad or that will provide the correct doubling.

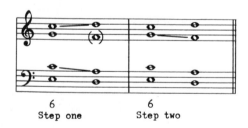

6   6
Step one   Step two

The above examples show proper placement when moving from a chord in first inversion to a second chord in root position. Now we shall examine the opposite situation. The following example shows a chord in root position followed by a second chord in first inversion.

- Move into the doubled tones by *contrary*, *oblique*, or *similar* motion. All voices should move by the smallest possible intervals.

- The remaining voice(s) should be moved to the nearest tone(s) that will complete the chord or that will provide correct doubling.

6   6

Step one   Step two

The use of a diminished chord is a special situation. It is often used in first inversion where it is strongest; root position and second inversion are seldom used.

- Double the bass (the third) of a diminished chord in first inversion.

When two or more chords in first inversion are used in succession, it may not be possible to use normal doubling. Irregularities of doubling can be used if they contribute to the smoothness of part writing, or must be used to avoid incorrect parallel motion.

Second inversions ($^6_4$) are not used as often as are first inversions or root positions; the bass should be doubled when the second inversion is used. Most chords in second inversion fall into one of four patterns: (1) cadential six-four; (2) passing six-four; (3) pedal six-four; and (4) arpeggio six-four.

1. The Cadential Six-Four Chord

The cadential six-four chord occurs at or close to a cadence. Many chords in second inversion occur as the result of the use of nonharmonic tones (tones which are not a regular part of the harmony), or they are used simply to delay resolution to a stronger chord.

- Cadential six-four chords occur on strong beats.
- Cadential six-four chords occur in one of two patterns: $I_4^6 - V$, or $IV_4^6 - I$.
- The upper voices (those which move as the six-four chord is resolved) move down by step.

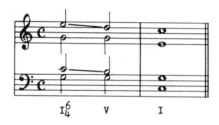

$$I_4^6 \qquad V \qquad I$$

2. The Passing Six-Four Chord

The passing six-four chord will either connect a chord in the first inversion with the same chord in root position, or the reverse.

- Passing six-four chords may appear between the root position and first inversion of any chord. But they are usually associated with the tonic or subdominant chords.

G Major I_6 $\quad$ v$_4^6$ $\quad$ I $\qquad$ G Minor iv $\quad$ i$_4^6$ $\quad$ iv$_6$

3. The Pedal Six-Four Chord

The pedal six-four chord will be less useful in vocal music than in instrumental music, but vocal music does often include the use of instruments. This chord is used over the same sustained or repeated bass note. It is used most often over the tonic, and the chords involved usually are tonic – subdominant – tonic.

I   IV$^6_4$ I

4. The Arpeggio Six-Four Chord

The arpeggio six-four chord most often falls on a weak beat, or the weak portion of a beat, and it is preceded by the same chord in first inversion or root position. It, like the pedal six-four chord, will be found when instruments are used.

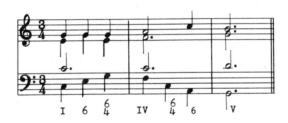

I   6 $^6_4$ IV $^6_4$ 6   V

Phrase Structure and Cadences

Music is organized into units (phrases) of various lengths. A usual phrase is four measures long, but phrases of two, three, five, or more measures can be found. The phrase ending provides breathing space for singers, and the phrase serves as the basic unit in the organization of music.

Cadences occur at the close of phrases. Cadences serve as points of repose, and they deserve special attention. There are four basic types of cadences:

- Authentic   V (or vii°) – I
- Plagal   IV – I
- Half   I, IV (or ii) – V; I – IV
- Deceptive   V – vi

The four basic types of cadences listed above may be grouped further as final and non-final cadences. Authentic and plagal cadences serve as final cadences, and half and deceptive cadences serve as non-final cadences.

- Final cadences (authentic and plagal) are capable of bringing the musical phrase to a complete close.
- Non-final cadences (half and deceptive) do not bring the music to a complete close. Non-final cadences require another phrase, or several phrases, to resolve their effect.

1. The Authentic Cadence

The authentic cadence occurs most frequently, and it is the strongest and most conclusive. It consists of V – I in major and V – i in minor. Not all authentic cadences exhibit the same degree of finality, for rhythm and voice placement must also be taken into consideration. The *perfect* authentic candence gives the greatest degree of finality, while the *imperfect* authentic cadence gives less finality. The terms *perfect* and *imperfect* describe the degree of finality of authentic cadences. The *perfect* authentic cadence includes (1) both chords in root position, and (2) the final tonic chord with the root in the soprano.

Perfect authentic cadence   Imperfect authentic cadence
(Bach—"Das neugenborne Kindelein")   (Final chord-third in soprano)

The perfect authentic cadence shown above also shows us an example of a *tièrce de Picardie* (Picardy third) in the final tonic chord. A Picardy third, B natural in the above example, causes what would otherwise be a minor tonic chord to become major.

While a viiº – I cadence is not often used at the close of a composition, it may have a place at the close of a phrase within a section. The following is an example of a viiº – I cadence, and it has been taken from the chorale of G.F. Handel, "Ach Gott und Herr, wie gross und schwer."

vii⁰₆ I

The leading tone triad (vii°) is not used as often as is the dominant. But it does have approximately the same function, and it may be substituted for the V chord.

2. The Plagal Cadence

The plagal cadence consists of IV – I and is the so-called "Amen" cadence that concludes many religious hymns. Just like authentic cadences, plagal cadences may be *perfect* or *imperfect*. A *perfect* plagal cadence has the root of the tonic chord in the soprano, and both the IV and I chords must be in root position.

IV   I

3. The Half Cadence

The half cadence is a non-final cadence, while the authentic and plagal cadences discussed above are final. The half cadence is used to conclude a musical phrase rather than to conclude a complete idea or composition. The half cadence appears most often as a I – V progression, but more rarely the IV chord may be used instead of the V.

I   V   I   IV

4. The Deceptive Cadence

The deceptive cadence is best understood by comparing it to the authentic cadence; the deceptive cadence occurs because another chord (usually the submediant) is substituted for the tonic chord in the authentic cadence. The deceptive cadence is a non-final cadence, and additional chords are required. Care should be taken, when working with a deceptive cadence in minor, not to have an augmented second appear in one of the voices. The deceptive cadence is quite effective in a minor key. Yet, sometimes additional interest or surprise is introduced because the submediant chord appears in major when it normally would have appeared in minor.

G: V   vi   F: V   VI

TECHNIQUES INVOLVED IN HARMONIZING

We have seen the principal options available at the most strategic points in the music, and we have seen the generally accepted practices that most arrangers and/or composers take into account. We have not discussed more general practices to be considered in harmonic progressions, but we now turn our attention to those points.

Primary chords (I, IV, V) furnish the main structural basis of a composition, but the basic use of those chords can be expanded by the use of secondary chords. Basically, there are two ways of expanding a I – IV – V – I progression: (1) move from a primary chord to its secondary chord before moving on to the next primary chord (a I – V – I progression may become I – vi – V – I); or (2) substitute a secondary chord for the usual primary chord (a I – IV – V – I progression may become I – ii – V – I).

There are many ways to harmonize a melody, but it will be best for the less experienced person to look first for one of three basic types of phrases:

- A phrase built on a single chord plus the cadence.
- A phrase based on harmonic embellishment of the tonic chord plus the cadence.
- A phrase in which the basic harmonic structure, or cadence formula, is distributed throughout the entire phrase.

Harmonizing a melody involves the selection of those chords that best suit the particular melody involved. Of course, there will be no one correct succession of chords, unless the melody is quite simple. But this is the point at which each person can exercise his own individual choices. We have already seen how it is possible to give variety and/or extend phrases by the use of secondary chords. Of course, those possibilities become more numerous in more complex music. We study examples from the music of recognized composers not so we can duplicate their music; we study the music of others who have been successful in order that we may know what common practice has been. After we have spend considerable time at that point, each one of us can develop our own individual style.

There are definite steps to follow in harmonizing a melody, and the techniques involved will be most useful for situations in which the melody is given. Therefore, in the following steps we are assuming the melody already has been given.

- Perform the melody often enough to become thoroughly acquainted with its motion.
- Determine the cadence(s) to be used.
- Remember that the phrase normally begins by emphasizing the tonic.
- Supply all possible harmonizations for the melody, giving priority to first selecting chords where there is particular emphasis. Where two or more chords are possible, every possibility should be considered before the full selection is made final.
- Choose the chords desired and outline the bass line, keeping in mind (1) some contrary motion between the soprano and bass parts is desirable, and (2) not all chords will normally be in root position. Some use of inversions will often allow the bass line to be more singable. Always check for parallel fifths and octaves.
- Complete the harmonization by writing the alto and tenor parts.

While the above steps give sufficient information for making proper choices in most situations, there will be harmonizations in which it will be necessary to repeat steps or go back to make changes. It should be stressed again that harmonic considerations are often a matter of individual choice. Until we gain considerable experience, we should try a particular harmonization in a laboratory situation before making final decisions.

THE USE OF NON-CHORD TONES

The previous discussion has concerned the use of generally accepted procedures for working with harmonic tones. Now we shall turn our attention to looking at some of the more often observed situations that utilize non-chord tones. Of course, non-chord tones are those which are not included as a part of the harmony. But we should recognize that everyone will not always agree that a particular tone is a chord or non-chord tone. In some situations, determining if a tone is a chord or non-chord tone depends upon the point of view of the one doing the analyzing. But, for our purposes, any tone which is not analyzed as part of the harmony is to be called a non-chord tone.

Non-chord tones are most often referred to by the way they are approached and left.

1. The type that is approached and left by step in the same direction is called a *passing tone*.

   • *Passing tones* may occur in one voice, or they may occur in more than one voice simultaneously.

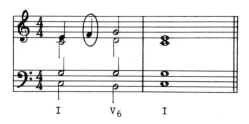

   • *Passing tones* may occur on accented or unaccented portions of the measure.

2. The type of non-chord tone that is approached and left by step with a change in direction is called a *neighboring tone*.

Bach – "Aus meines Herzens Grunde"

- A *neighboring tone* may either be above or below the pitch to which it is related. It moves from and returns to the same pitch.
- A *neighboring tone* may occur in one voice, or more than one may occur in two or more voices simultaneously.
- *Neighboring tones* usually (but not always) occur on the weak portion of the measure.

3. The type of non-chord tone that is approached by leap and left by step is called an *appoggiatura*.

- It should be emphasized that the *appoggiatura* is approached by leap. If approached from above, the note which follows will be a step above; if approached from below, the note which follows will be a step below.
- An *appoggiatura* most often (but not always) occurs on a stressed portion of the measure.
- Those which occur in two voices simultaneously are called *double appoggiaturas*.

4. The type of non-chord tone that is approached by step and which leaves by leap (generally with a change of direction) is called an *escape tone*.

    (This is the opposite of the *appoggiatura*.)

Bach – "Gott des Himmels und der Erden"

- The most usual circumstance is to ascend by step followed by a descending leap, but the reverse may also occur.

- Those which occur in two voices simultaneously are called *double escape tones*.

5. A type of non-chord tone that is approached by step and left by repetition is called an *anticipation*. It has been described as a premature sounding of the following tone, which is a chord tone.

- It is possible to approach an *anticipation* from above or below.

6. A type of non-chord tone that is approached by the same tone and left by step is called a *suspension*.

- It is possible to resolve a *suspension* upward or downward. But those that resolve downward are more usual.

- The preparatory tone often is tied to the suspended tone, but the suspended tone may be sounded individually. (Those that are sounded individually may be called an *appoggiatura*.)

- The preparation often (but not always) is two times the length of the *suspension*.
- *Suspensions* often are classified by using figured bass symbols such as 4 − 3 and 2 − 3. In the 4 − 3 *suspension*, the interval of a fourth exists between the lowest part and the *suspension*, and the interval of a third exists between the bass and the resolution.

AN INTRODUCTION TO SEVENTH CHORDS

Previous discussion has been concerned with the use of triad and non-chord tones, and such basic information is important to any writing of music. But it is now common practice to add interest by using seventh chords. A seventh chord consists of four tones; it consists of the usual three tones of a triad plus a fourth note added a third above the fifth of the triad. Seventh chords bring greater tonal variety and an added urgency of resolution to music, and their use is no longer new or unusual. The seventh chord contains an interval of a seventh between the root and seventh of the chord. Seventh chords may be built on any scale step.

Seventh chords may be identified as minor, major, diminished, and/or augmented. Of these, the major and/or minor are used most commonly. These terms are used to identify (1) the type of triad, and (2) the type of interval between the root and seventh.

Major   Major-Minor   Minor-Major   Minor   Diminished   Augmented-Major

The dominant seventh chord is by far the most often used seventh chord, and it usually progresses to the tonic or submediant triad.

Brahams – *Ein deutsches Requiem*

The dominant seventh chord in the preceding example is major-minor. It consists of (1) the interval of a seventh between the root and seventh of the chord, and (2) the tritone (three whole tones) which occurs between the third and seventh of the chord (B-flat to E-natural). Notice that each tone of the tritone resolves outward by half-step. An augmented fourth tends to resolve outward, while the tones of a diminished fifth tend to resolve inward; this follows usual practice of inactive tones moving toward active tones.

- the *supertonic* moves to the *tonic* (2 to 1)
- the *mediant* moves to the *subdominant* (3 to 4)
- the *submediant* moves to the *dominant* (6 to 5)
- the *leading tone* moves to the *tonic* (7 to 1)

Proper resolution of the tritone may lead to irregular doubling, but it is important to resolve active tones according to their natural tendency. The seventh of the dominant seventh (4th scale step) has a strong tendency to resolve downward.

Much more freedom is possible in the approach to the seventh than in its resolution. However, most sevenths occur in patterns that relate to certain types of non-chord tones.

Chords of the dominant seventh may be used in all positions. But, when the seventh or third is in the soprano or bass, its natural melodic tendency is not to be violated.

SOME COMMENTS ABOUT ALTERED NON-CHORD TONES AND SECONDARY DOMINANTS

The use of altered non-chord tones and secondary dominants can add color and variety to a composition that is essentially diatonic. While these elements should be used less often than those more basic elements discussed previously, altered non-chord tones may be included without difficulty in what is otherwise basic writing. Secondary dominants may occur as the result of a shift of the dominant function to other degrees of the scale.

An altered non-chord tone is different from the seven basic tones of a particular key, and the two most often found are the *raised fourth* and *lowered seventh* degrees. The *raised fourth* occurs in both major and minor, and the *lowered seventh* occurs in major.

In minor, the most often found altered non-chord tones are as given below. The black note is the altered non-chord tone, and the whole note is the tone to which the altered tone most often progresses.

The following altered non-chord tones may be found in major along with the more prevalent *raised fourth* and *lowered seventh*. Again, the black note is the altered non-chord tone, and the whole note is the tone to which it most often progresses.

The use of chromatic alterations may result in two or more passing tones in succession. Also, two or more altered non-chord tones may occur simultaneously.

Secondary Dominants

While quite a variety of altered chords is possible, secondary dominants are the most often used. It is usually simply a dominant chord in the dominant key; it may be used in any position. For example, a usual V^7 chord in the key of C major is G-B-D-F; a secondary dominant (the dominant of the dominant key) is D-F-sharp-A-C. The secondary dominant does not change the basic key of C major, but it does give added color to a

composition that otherwise may be too traditional. Notice the handling of
the secondary dominant in the following musical example,

Bach – "Ach Gott, wie manches Herzeleid"

The real function of secondary dominants is to add color and increase
motion within the musical phrase. They give the music added temporary
tension, and they increase the status of the diatonic triads to which they
resolve. While their use is a step beyond the most basic of harmonies, the
use of secondary dominants should be within the grasp of anyone who
writes or arranges choral music.

MODULATION TO CLOSELY RELATED KEYS

We have discussed the use of non-chord tones and secondary dominants, and it has been stated that they may be used to add color to the
existing key. But their use does not move the composition from the original
key. The following discussion gives information that will be helpful when
modulating to closely related keys.

Modulation may be said to have taken place when a new tonic has
been established and when your ear accepts that a new tonal center has
been established. A new key may be established by (1) the use of a common chord, (2) chromatic modulation, or (3) diatonic modulation.

Since we are concerned at this point only with closely related keys, it
is appropriate to comment on what is meant by that phrase. Briefly, closely
related keys are those in which the key signatures differ from one another
by only one sharp or flat. Any given key has five closely related keys. For
example, the closely related keys of C major are (1) *a* minor, (2) F major,
(3) *d* minor, (4) G major, and (5) *e* minor.

Common Chord

This method gives a smooth transition to the new key by the use of a pivot chord that functions as an integral part of both keys. The actual change is accomplished by using a dominant in the new key, and, if it is considered alone, this chord may be called a secondary dominant. Modulation to the new key is confirmed by the use of chords that are a part of the new key, or by a cadence. The common chord immediately precedes the dominant chord, and it is the dominant chord (or the leading tone triad) that moves the music into the new key. The following music shows one example as used by Bach in his chorale: "Ach Gott, wie manches Herzleid."

The following observations apply to situations in which modulation is accomplished by employing the common chord.

- It is the dominant chord (leading tone triad or seventh chord) of the new key that moves the composition out of the former key.
- It is the common chord (common to both keys) that provides a stepping-stone to the dominant chord, and it most often is the first chord preceding the dominant chord.
- Since the common chord often precedes the dominant chord of the new key, it will often be either a subdominant or supertonic chord of the new key.
- If neither the subdominant nor the supertonic of the new key is available to use as the common chord, either the tonic or submediant chord is quite acceptable.

Diatonic Modulation

This type of modulation occurs when (1) there is diatonic melodic movement in all voices, and when (2) the common chord is diatonic in both the old and the new keys. Diatonic modulation makes use only of chords that are diatonic in both keys. There is no chromatic movement immediately preceding or following the common chord.

Chromatic Modulation

Chromatic movement in one or more voices leading to the movement from one key to another is defined as chromatic modulation. Most modulations involve the use of a common chord, but, when it includes chromatic motion, it is called chromatic modulation.

Bach – "Das neugeborne Kindelein"

In summary, the use of basic harmonic practices as commonly accepted today will tend to result in standard, traditional writing. These practices are important to any editor, arranger, or composer of choral music, and this chapter has included discussions of many of the most often used techniques.

11

Advanced and/or Modern
Music Writing Techniques

There are numerous ways to add tonal variety to a musical phrase and some of those ways were discussed in the previous chapter. But your writing will be more interesting if you use additional techniques. This, the final chapter, will show additional ways to add color to your writing. Since most choirs now perform music in non-traditional notation as well as more traditional scores, a portion of this chapter will be devoted to a presentation of basic practices in choral compositions which include non-traditional notation.

USES FOR BORROWED CHORDS

Chords that belong to one key but are actually used in a parallel key are known as borrowed chords. Such an additional use further expands available harmonic resources and tends to add color to basic chord progressions. Since the sixth and seventh scale steps of the melodic minor scale are different when they ascend than when they descend, there are more chords available in minor keys than are available in major keys. For this reason, it is usual to find more use of borrowed chords when the composition is in a major key than when it is in a minor key.

The only borrowed chord to be useful in minor is the tonic chord of the parallel major, and this chord occurs most often at the cadence where the major quality may be preferred to the more usual minor. In such a situation, the final chord contains a *Picardy third*.

It is important to distinguish between a change of mode and an actual modulation. Modulation involves a change in key center, but a change of mode only involves a change from major to minor or the reverse. When one moves from a major key (for example: C major) to establish the tonal center in the relative minor (*a* minor), modulation has taken place; but when the move is from a major key (C major) to the parallel minor (*c* minor), there has been a change of mode.

Borrowed chords are to be treated as having the same function as does the usual chord of the predominant key. For example, a IV chord still progresses to the V, I, or II. The use of borrowed chords is not greatly different, but to include them in a composition does give the possibility of a greater variety of tone color. The most common borrowed chords in major are as follows.

It should be emphasized again that borrowed chords, such as those shown in the above example, should be thought of as progressing in the same way as do the regular unaltered chords of the key being used. Borrowed chords have been a part of music vocabulary for several centuries and their use does add greater variety to a composition.

Mass in C Major
K.317

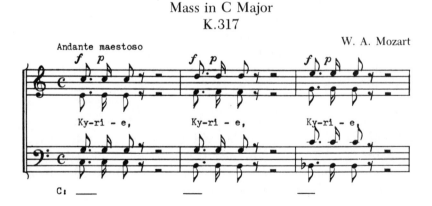

Ky - ri - e   e - le - i - son.

AUGMENTED SIXTH CHORDS

Augmented sixth chords are so categorized because of the interval of an augmented sixth that occurs between the bass and an upper part when the chords are in their most common position. While the notes of these chords are built in thirds, chromatic alteration also has an important place. The actual written root no longer retains its important position in the augmented sixth chord; it surrenders its influence to another chord tone that functions, or sounds, as the root.

There are three types of augmented sixth chords: (1) the *Italian Sixth*, (2) the *German Sixth*, and (3) the *French Sixth*. Examples of these three chords are shown below, and you should be aware that each chord contains intervals of a major third and an augmented sixth above the lowest note.

Italian Sixth   German Sixth   French Sixth

- In the *Italian Sixth* chord, the major third above the bass is often doubled by the fourth voice part.
- In the *German Sixth* chord, the intervals above the bass include the major third and perfect fifth.
- In the *French Sixth* chord, the intervals above the bass include a major third and an augmented fourth.

While augmented sixth chords may be built in thirds above the bass note, in this position the lowest note does not sound as the root of the chord. Therefore, this position is recommended less than the one following. While augmented sixth chords may be found in any position, the most recommended position is to have the interval of an augmented sixth between the bass and an upper part. Most often that augmented sixth expands outward to the octave.

Perfect fifth may occur when the *German Sixth* progresses directly to the dominant, but they are usually avoided or disguised by the melody. On the first two counts, last measure, of the following example, successive augmented sixth chords are shown as they were used by Schubert; the chord on count one is a *German Sixth*, and the chord on the second count is an *Italian Sixth*.

Mass in G Major, "Sanctus"

The following general observations apply to augmented sixth chords as a group.

- Most such chords are constructed on the sixth scale degree in harmonic minor, or the lowered sixth scale step in major.
- They usually resolve to the dominant, and they are quite active chords. When a secondary dominant resolves to a chord other than the dominant, it is generally part of a very chromatic style of writing.
- When these chords are based on the lowered second degree of the scale, they usually resolve to the tonic chord in root position. In such a situation, the interval of the augmented sixth follows the usual practice of expanding outward to the octave.
- When these chords are based on the fourth degree of the major scale, they usually resolve to the tonic chord in root position.

- The most common use of such a chord is to highlight the appearance of a dominant chord by providing a chromatic approach to it.

THE NEAPOLITAN SIXTH

The *Neapolitan Sixth* chord is really an altered supertonic triad; it is a major triad built on the lowered second scale step either in major or minor. It usually appears in the first inversion and in such a position its symbol is N^6. The *Neapolitan Sixth* may be used in root position or second inversion. But since the first inversion is most recommended, the following examples show the chord in its most usual position.

Since the N^6 chord is an altered supertonic chord, it normally progresses to the dominant chord. It produces added color, and this effect is most evident when the N^6 (*Neapolitan Sixth*) chord is followed at once by the dominant chord. But other chords may be used between the N^6 and the dominant: (1) a secondary dominant may be used between these two chords, or (2) a tonic six-four chord may be used between the N^6 and the following dominant chord. The N^6 chord should not be considered to be as active as are many other altered chords.

MODULATION TO REMOTE KEYS

Two different keys whose signatures differ from one another by more than one sharp or flat are called remote, or distant keys. Techniques used to modulate to remote keys are also applicable when modulating to closely related keys. But those techniques discussed here are most closely associated with modulating to remote keys. Such modulations give greater tonal variety than do modulations to closely related keys, because remote keys have fewer tones in common.

While parallel major and minor keys have key signatures that differ by three sharps or flats, their identity is quite close because they share the same tonic, subdominant, and dominant tones. Their differences relate to quality rather than to key; therefore, we do not refer to movement between parallel major and minor keys as modulation. Modulation involves a shift of tonality from one basic pitch to another.

The process of common chord modulation has already been discussed to some degree, and, in such a modulation, the common chord is unaltered in each of the two keys involved. Altered chords are useful in moving from one remote key to another, but they may also have a place in moving from one closely related key to another. Diminished seventh and major-minor seventh chords are quite useful, and the diminished seventh chord is particularly important. The diminished seventh chord can be written in four different ways, as follows, with each of the four pitches serving as the root.

In the following example, there is modulation from the key of A major to b minor.

Bach – "Was mein Gott will, das g'scheh' allzeit"

NINTH, ELEVENTH, AND THIRTEENTH CHORDS

Chords are built on intervals of a third. Two superimposed intervals of a third produce a triad, and three produce a seventh chord. It is quite possible to continue with this construction to chords which contain four, five, or six intervals of a third; these chords are called ninth, eleventh, and thirteenth chords respectively. They are used only when colorful effects are desired.

These chords may occur on any degree of the scale, but most often they are seen as dominant chords. As is shown in the above example, ninth, eleventh, and thirteenth chords contain five or more tones. They seldom appear as complete chords, and there are several general observations which apply to ninth chords in particular.

- The fifth of the chord is usually omitted.
- It usually appears in root position.
- The ninth is at least an interval of a ninth above the root, and it usually is in the highest part.
- There are two types of dominant ninth chords: (1) the major ninth chord, which consists of a major-minor seventh chord plus a major ninth, and (2) the minor ninth chord which consists of a major-minor seventh chord plus a minor ninth.

The eleventh chord may be seen as adding another interval of a third above a ninth chord. Two tones must be omitted when one is writing for four parts. Those two omitted parts are usually the third, and either the fifth or ninth of the chord.

Lastly, a thirteenth chord consists of six superimposed thirds. When one writes for four parts, three of these chord tones must be omitted. There are several possibilities for choosing tones to be omitted, but one point should always be observed—the third and the eleventh are not present at the same time. If the third of the chord is used, the eleventh will certainly not be included, and the reverse is also true.

Extensive use of ninth, eleventh, and thirteenth chords tend to obscure rather than to clarify writing in the traditional sense. Since the complete thirteenth chord, for example, includes all seven tones of a diatonic scale, even the tonal center may be obscured. But these chords have their legitimate place when you are working with impressionistic music, or music that can be set for a modern sound.

EDITIONS, ARRANGEMENTS AND COMPOSITIONS

The establishing of standards for published choral music has been long delayed, but recently there has been a real effort to distribute a statement that could help to eliminate many of the problems that have existed. Too often, we still find music that does not accurately reflect the original notation or intention of the composer; this is particularly a problem when we look for a published score of an early composition. It appears to be self-evident that a choral conductor should be concerned that the music he conducts is as authentic as is possible. Certainly, we all have seen two or more editions of the same work that are so different in published form that they could be mistaken for different compositions. I once purchased editions of the Heinrich Schütz *Passions* that called for the use of instruments. Such editions are, of course, extreme examples of bad editing practices, but those particular editions were sold over the counter and performed for many years.

Within recent years, the Choral Editing Standards Committee of the American Choral Directors Association formulated a statement that set down minimum standards. The following quotation is taken from the statement on "Minimum Standards of Editorial Practice" as originally printed in the *American Choral Review*.[1] These ten points are excerpts taken from the full statement.

1. The sources used in preparing the edition should be identified. If the source is a recognized scholarly edition . . . many of the following procedures may be eliminated, providing always that it is identified as such and changes from it are specified.

2. All original material, including the original composer, title, opus number, and instrumentation of the composition should be supplied, as well as such matters as figured bass numbers and original realizations. Where piano-vocal score format is necessary, a description of the original instrumentation should be included.

3. The original text should be provided with the music, as well as any translations or adaptations, and the author, translator, source, and liturgical use of the text should be identified wherever possible.

4. All editorial changes in and additions to the original sources must be clearly distinguishable.

5. Where necessary, rhythmic values, rhythmic groupings, accents, pitch levels, clefs, time signatures, key signatures, and other notation should be modernized. When such changes are made, an incipit showing the original notation should be included, and a description of the alterations not shown by the incipit be supplied in an editorial note.

6. Where two different editions must be used together—as in the case of separate choral and instrumental parts—every effort should be made to assist the performer to identify and rectify differences between them.

[1]Collins, Walter S., "Choral Editing Standards—A Report," *American Choral Review*, XII, No. 1, p. 26.

7. The composer's dates and the date of the composition should be given where shown. It is more desirable to provide musical and historical information about the piece itself and its performance than biographical information about the composer, which is easily obtainable elsewhere.

8. Measure numbers or rehearsal letters should be provided to assist the rehearsal. In order to stimulate more musical rehearsing, such markings should be placed at convenient stopping and starting points in the music, rather than by some arbitrary system. . . .

9. The entire text and any translation should be printed straight through in easily readable form before the piece in order that it may be read and understood as a whole.

10. An estimated time of performance should be provided.

To more clearly distinguish between an *edition*, a *transcription*, an *arrangement*, and an original composition, may be helpful in your search for new repertoire.

- An *arrangement* is usually clearly identified as such on the performing score; it is changed in some definite way from the original music. Several different terms and phrases may be used to identify this type of publication, but there usually is an indication such as "arranged by." This type of publication may include changes such as arranging instrumental music for chorus or making a setting of a solo song for chorus. It may indicate a changing of the text. As a group, arrangements often differ greatly from the original.

- An *edition* should serve as an authoritative presentation of a composition. An *edition* should include, as nearly as possible, the composer's original work. An *edition* should show quite clearly all deviations from the original, and the editor should be careful to clearly list his own ideas as distinguished from those original indications included by the composer.

- A *transcription* is a reproduction of an original composition, but with a change of notation. A *transcription* of choral music most often is a reproduction of an early composition. But the use of the term in choral music should not be confused with its use in the instrumental field. In modern instrumental music, a *transcription* is said to be a rewriting of a composition for another performing medium. This term will be less appropriate to the field of choral music than are *arrangement* and *edition*.

Unless the printed score contains an indication that the music is an *edition*, an *arrangement*, or a *transcription*, it is understood that the music is an original composition.

SOME COMMENTS ABOUT ARRANGING

Although there may be a place for simple inspiration, it will be of basic importance to begin the process of arranging a choral composition with a plan in mind. At first, it will be best to choose original music which is melodically and harmonically uncomplicated. It may be an obvious point, but you should try to make the harmony as full as is possible, even in a unison or two-part arrangement. Any rewritten parts should be kept as close to the original as is possible, and awkward skips and progressions should be avoided. Most arrangements are approached with the idea of simplifying the music in some way, but it should always be kept in mind that the most important single factor in arranging is good part writing.

It will be helpful for the person with relatively little experience to consider the following points when first considering this matter of arranging choral music.

- Take into consideration the type of group that will perform the completed musical score, and, if possible, also consider the actual performance circumstances.
- Relatively simple music well performed is preferred to a more complex arrangement inadequately performed.
- In many instances, it will be helpful to know the actual voices that will sing the music. Give particular attention to the part you will write for the weakest section of the choir.
- Achieve a thorough knowledge of music and text of the original composition.
- Determine the approximate dimension of the arrangement.
- Outline the preliminary structure of the arrangement before you actually begin to set the music down on paper.
- Sketch various themes in different ways before making final decisions. Determine if the principal theme is strong enough to fill such an important position.
- Will the principal theme best be set with a harmonized, rhythmic, or arpeggiated accompaniment?
- Will the principal thematic material best be set in the top voice, or should it be placed in an inner voice part?

- Are any changes of key, tempo, or meter suggested by the original music?

If you are arranging for your own choir, or a choir you know very well, it will be helpful to make a comprehensive chart such as the following. A full understanding of the different possible sounds involved can bring you even closer to the various sonorities present in your choir.

Additional Voicings of the C major Chord:[2]

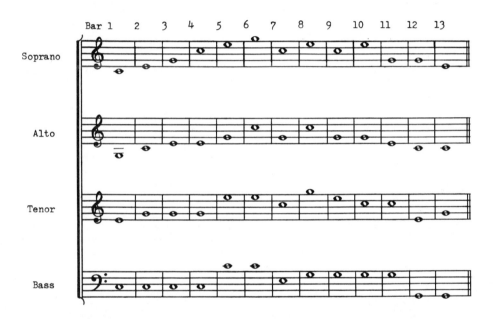

You will find it helpful to have your singers move through this series of sonorities carefully; such an exercise will let you hear their voices in different circumstances and it will also let your singers hear themselves more carefully. You should notice that the first measure shows the voices in closed position and every succeeding measure has some change in position and tessitura. Such a chart can be constructed for any chord, and to use this method for becoming particularly acquainted with the sound of your singers when they perform the most important chords of your arrangement can be very helpful.

---

[2]Kerr, Anita, *Voices* (N.Y.: MCA Music, 1972), p. 3.

The following series is also taken from a chart used by Anita Kerr, and it can be equally helpful as a representative example for seventh chords.[3]

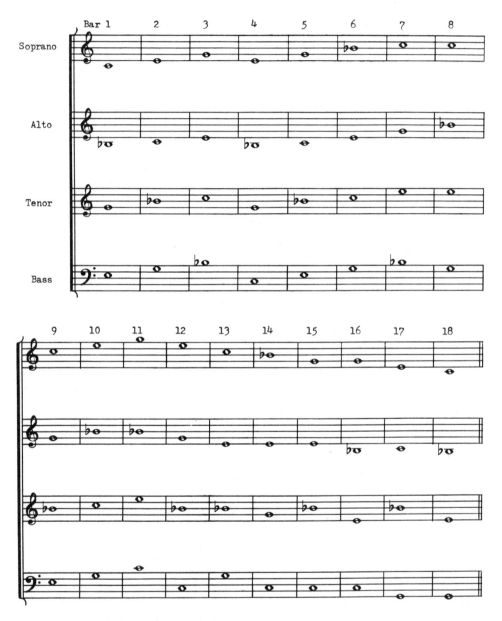

This third chart illustrates possible uses of sonorities within more complex chords.[4]

---

[3]Ibid., p. 4.
[4]Ibid., p. 6.

Use notes 1, 3, 5, 7 flat, 9 and 11.

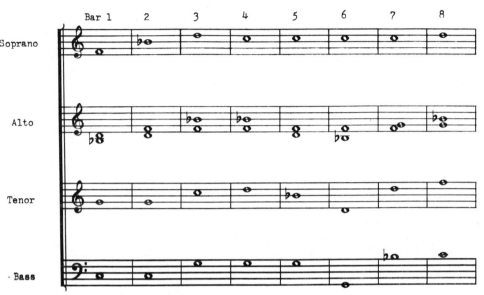

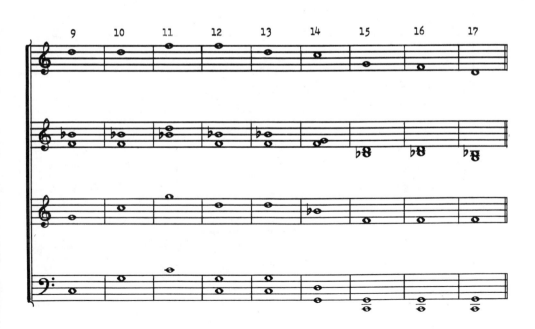

If you absorb the steps listed early in this discussion, and if you examine each of the most important chords in your arrangement as has been shown in the preceding representative examples, you will have a good start in knowing how to work with the basics of the craft. After you are confident that you have a grasp of those preceding materials, you should become acquainted with more music. It is not necessarily the same thing to look at choral music from the point of view of a conductor and from the point of view of a writer. If you really wish to know how different combinations of voices sound, examine and perform all types of choral music; then try to write your own arrangement or composition. While it is not possible to show an example of every type here, the following examples are well

Sure On This Shining Night

Samuel Barber

Copyright © 1941, 1961 by G. Schirmer, Inc.
(Used by Permission)

done, and they represent substantial music which is not at all technically difficult. It will be well for you to choose music that is not complex before you try to work with more advanced compositions. The following serve as models.

"Sure on this shining night" was originally a solo song by Samuel Barber, and it has been performed many times as an art song. But Barber, himself, also set this lovely melody and text for chorus. It will be both interesting and educational if you will perform just the soprano line and piano accompaniment first, and then perform the alto, tenor, and bass parts in turn. You should personally hear and experience each line by means of your own performance before you give the music to your choir; then you will hear the total effect. But the first experience (and perhaps the most important experience) will best be your own singing. Ultimately, you should listen to your singers perform two or more parts in as many combinations as is possible. This time will be well spent, for all persons involved will become quite well aware of the unique purpose of each different part of the score.

The second example shows an octavo chorus as taken from "The Imperial" Mass by Haydn and as arranged by Charles C. Hirt. While space cannot be expanded to show a portion of the original score here, you are encouraged to compare the following excerpt with Haydn's score.

Kyrie Eleison
From "The Imperial" Mass
by Joseph Haydn

Arranged by
Charles C. Hirt

© 1957 WARNER BROS. INC.
All Rights Reserved
(Used by Permission)

You are encouraged to examine arrangements included in your present performance library, and you are encouraged not to perform those which depart greatly from the original intent of the composer. We in the choral field have been guilty of using bad arrangements much too often, and one of the most progressive decisions we can make is to eliminate such music from our concert programs. Perhaps you can make a better arrangement yourself. In my view, the position we take should be to continue to use arrangements, but to take much more care in being certain to use those that faithfully reproduce the original intent of the composer.

NON-TRADITIONAL NOTATION

An increasing number of choral compositions call for the singers to produce non-traditional sounds. We have discussed traditional theoretical techniques and compositional practices in some detail, and those considerations are valid for most of the choral music being sung today. But, an increasing amount of twentieth-century choral music requires singers to produce sounds that are sometimes not within the more usual bounds of good tone production. A choral singer today who sings a large quantity of music should expect, at some point, to be asked to produce a wide variety of sounds in addition to the standard and time-honored sounds derived from traditional notational systems and/or a specific language.

The following notational examples are based, in large part, on information included in the handbook of Frank Pooler and Brent Pierce.[5] The sounds included here are in regular use today, and they are presented with the intention of helping to standardize common practice in this new field.

such notation indicates that the rhythm specified is to be sung on an approximate pitch. Singers who are accustomed to traditional notation may have considerable difficulty in adjusting to such a requirement.

this is another way to notate the requirement that the singers perform approximate pitches.

the absence of a note head indicates an indefinite pitch.

this music is to be spoken on the assigned pitch.

to be murmured on various pitches.

to be spoken on various pitches.

the thickness of the letter indicates the relative dynamics to be used.

this notation indicates the use of a whisper.

▲ ▼ the pitch is to be performed as high (▲) or as low(▼) as is possible. These signs are frequently used together:

▶ ◀ such signs indicate the performer is to inhale (▶) or exhale (◀).

the preceding sign indicates a tongue click is to be used.

■ the performer is to cough.

? or ⌐'⌐ when such signs are included, the performer is to use a glottal stroke.

---

[5]Pooler, Frank and Pierce, Brent, *New Choral Notation* (N.Y.: Walton Music Corporation), 1971, pp. i-viii.

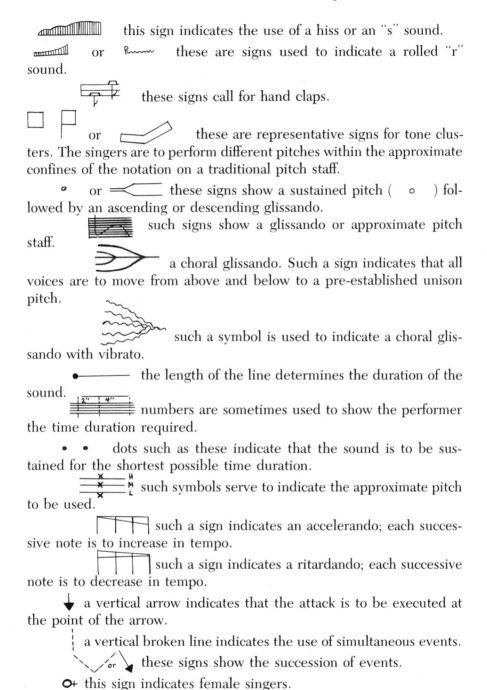 this sign indicates the use of a hiss or an "s" sound.

or these are signs used to indicate a rolled "r" sound.

these signs call for hand claps.

or these are representative signs for tone clusters. The singers are to perform different pitches within the approximate confines of the notation on a traditional pitch staff.

or these signs show a sustained pitch (o) followed by an ascending or descending glissando.

such signs show a glissando or approximate pitch staff.

a choral glissando. Such a sign indicates that all voices are to move from above and below to a pre-established unison pitch.

such a symbol is used to indicate a choral glissando with vibrato.

the length of the line determines the duration of the sound.

numbers are sometimes used to show the performer the time duration required.

• • dots such as these indicate that the sound is to be sustained for the shortest possible time duration.

such symbols serve to indicate the approximate pitch to be used.

such a sign indicates an accelerando; each successive note is to increase in tempo.

such a sign indicates a ritardando; each successive note is to decrease in tempo.

a vertical arrow indicates that the attack is to be executed at the point of the arrow.

a vertical broken line indicates the use of simultaneous events.

these signs show the succession of events.

this sign indicates female singers.

this sign indicates male singers.

the sound is to be sustained until the breath is exhausted.

the sound is to be sustained until the breath is exhausted and there is to be a continuous decrescendo.

† raise the pitch a quarter tone.

♯ raise the pitch three quarter tones.

♭ lower the pitch a quarter tone.

♭ lower the pitch three quarter tones.

—·—·—· such a seccession indicates repetition by the entire group.

∞ the mark of infinity shown above a repeat sign, for example, indicates that the section can be repeated as often as desired.

⌒ this sign signifies that the rhythmic values need not be observed.

CONSIDERATIONS WHEN WORKING
WITH CHORAL MUSIC AND TAPE

Including a tape in the choral field adds a dimension not ordinarily encountered. Such an addition may be viewed as adding to (or taking away from) the usual performance resources. A prepared tape may give an added sound dimension, but it also may take away from the flexibility many performers have learned to expect. It is quite important for the performer to know exact metronomic markings, for the prepared tape is not flexible. If the correct performance tempo is known from the beginning, it will be possible for the conductor and singers to prepare more carefully and intelligently for the actual performance.

The giving of pitch cues can be another problem, for the accompanying sounds are non-traditional. Because of this, it may be necessary to use the sound of bells, or a pedal sound, to give the pitch sufficiently for your singers to be comfortable.

While you should expect to use more rehearsal time in preparing your first few choral compositions with tape, including such experiences in your choral repertoire will add to the variety of new music that you introduce to your performers and audiences. While the great compositions of the past will be (and should be) performed for many years to come, we cannot expect to maintain an up-to-date program unless we also use new ideas and techniques such as are shown here. It is an adventure you should not miss.

Appendix *I*

Compliance with the Copyright Law

INQUIRY FORM ON OUT-OF-PRINT COPYRIGHTED MUSIC

Prepared by: Music Publisher's Association of the United States, and
National Music Publishers' Association Inc.

INSTRUCTIONS

This form is to be prepared in duplicate. After completing the boxed section and signing both copies where indicated, forward them to the publisher who will complete the form and return it to you. If the publisher indicates a payment for the right you request, and if the conditions are agreeable to you, remit the amount to the publisher together with the original copy, which he will have signed, whereupon the agreement will be completed.

To:_____
            (Name of Publisher)

Address:_____

_____

I (We) wish to procure _____ copies of your copyrighted publication:

_____
           (Title)   (Arrangement)

by:_____

If it is in print:
Please indicate the price per copy here _____

If it is out of print:
A) Do you have plans to reprint it? _____ If so, when? _____

    At what price per copy? _____

B) If there are no plans for reprinting I (we) request your permission to have a non-exclusive right to reproduce by photocopy_____ copies for use by my (our)

_____
          (students, members, congregation, etc.)

(see over)

As consideration for your permission to do so, I (we) will pay you in advance of making the copies_____per copy, totalling $_____.

The copies will be identical to your publication including the copyright notice. The following will be legibly included on the first page of each copy of our reproduction:

> "This reproduction is made with the express consent
> of _____
> (copyright owner's name)
> in accordance with the provisions of the United States
> Copyright Law."

I (We) acknowledge that I (we) are granted no right to sell, loan or otherwise distribute reproduced copies of the publication other than for the use set down above. No other rights of any kind for any other use are included in this permission.

If you do not grant the above permission, will you supply me (us) with _____ photocopies?_____If so, at what price per copy?_____

_____

By:_____

Accepted and Agreed to: Address:_____

_____

_____Date: _____

STANDARD FORM RECOMMENDED BY:

Music Educators National Conference, Music Teachers National Association, National Association of Jazz Educators, National Association of Schools of Music, Music Publishers' Association of the USA and National Music Publishers' Association.

REQUEST FOR PERMISSION TO ARRANGE
PART I
INSTRUCTIONS

This form is to be prepared in duplicate. After completing Part I and signing both copies where indicated, forward both to the publisher who will complete Part II of the form and return it to you. If the publisher indicates a payment for the right you request, and if the conditions are agreeable to you, remit the amount to the publisher together with the original copy, which he will have signed, whereupon the agreement will be completed.

To:_____Date:_____
                     (Name of Publisher)

_____
                     (Address of Publisher)

Gentlemen:

   We hereby request your permission and non-exclusive license to arrange the following musical composition:

                     _____

        By:_____(words)

              _____(music)

(hereinafter referred to as "The Arrangement")

1. The Arrangement will be for_____in
                                         (type of arrangement)

_____. We will produce
              (number of instrumental and/or vocal parts)

_____copies of The Arrangement for use and performance only by our

_____for which no admission fees shall be charged,
     (teachers, students, members, congregation, etc.)

or for performance otherwise exempt under the provision of the U.S. Copyright Law.

2. No right to record or to reproduce additional copies is granted to us. We understand that if we wish to record The Arrangement a separate license will be required. We agree not to distribute (except for use of copies as provided in Paragraph 1), sell, loan or lease copies of The Arrangement to anyone.

PART II

3. All copies of The Arrangement shall bear the following copyright notice and the words "Arranged by Permission":

at the bottom of the first page of music of each part of The Arrangement. We will furnish you with a copy of The Arrangement upon completion.

(over)

4. We will have The Arrangement made by a person connected with us as our employee for hire, without any payment obligation on your part, and our signature below, together with yours underneath the words "Permission Granted" below shall assign to you all of our right in The Arrangement and the copyright in The Arrangement together with the sole right of registering the copyright as a work made for hire in your name or the name of your designee.

5. Additional provisions (if applicable):

6. In consideration of your permission to arrange, we will pay you $_____ upon the granting by you of the permission requested.

7. This license agreement sets forth our entire understanding and may not be modified or amended except by written agreement signed by both of us.

Very truly yours,

_____
Name of institution

_____
Address

By:_____

Permission Granted:

By:_____
    Publisher

Permission denied because:

☐ 1. Arrangement available for sale.

☐ 2. Arrangement in process of publication for sale.

☐ 3. May not be arranged because of contractual commitments.

☐ 4. Other:_____

_____

Appendix II

Selected Publishers of Choral Music

Alexander Broude, Inc.
225 West 57th Street
New York, N.Y. 10019

American Composers Alliance
170 West 74th Street
New York, N.Y. 10023

Arista
Box 1596
Brooklyn, N.Y. 11201

Associated Music Publishers
609 Fifth Avenue
New York, N.Y. 10017

Augsburg Publishing House
426 South 5th Street
Minneapolis, Minnesota 55415

B. F. Wood
1790 Broadway
New York City 10019

Bärenreiter Verlag
Heinrich Schütz Allee 29-37
55 Kassel-Wilhelmeshohe, Germany

Belwin-Mills Publishing Corp.
26 Deshon Drive
Melville, N.Y. 11746

Boosey and Hawkes, Inc.
Lawson Boulevard
Oceanside, N.Y. 11572

Boston Music Company
116 Boylston Street
Boston, Mass. 02116

Bourne Company
1212 Avenue of the Americas
New York, N.Y. 10036

Carl Fischer, Inc..
62 Cooper Square
New York, N.Y. 10003

Choral Art Publications
1540 Broadway
New York, N.Y. 10036

Colombo, Frank
16 West 61st Street
New York, N.Y. 10023

Concordia Publishing House
3558 South Jefferson Avenue
St. Louis, Missouri 63118

Durand and Company
Presser Place
Bryn Mawr, Pennsylvania 19010

E. B. Marks Music Corp.
1790 Broadway
New York, N.Y. 10019

E. C. Schirmer Music Co.
112 South Street
Boston, Mass. 02111

Elkan-Vogel, Inc.
Presser Place
Bryn Mawr, Pennsylvania 19010

Frank Music Corp.
119 West 57th Street
New York, N.Y. 10019

G. Schirmer, Inc.
866 Third Avenue
New York, N.Y. 10022

Galaxy Music Corp.
2121 Broadway
New York, N.Y. 10023

H. W. Gray Company, Inc,
c/o Belwin-Mills
25 Deshon Drive
Melville, N.Y. 11746

Harold Flammer, Inc.
c/o Shawnee Press
Delaware Water Gap,
Pennsylvania 18237

Joseph Boonin, Inc.
P.O. Box 2124
South Hackensack, N.J. 07606

Lawson-Gould Music Publishers
866 Third Avenue
New York, N.Y. 10022

Mark Foster Music Company
P.O. Bos 4012
Champaign, Illinois 61820

Mercury Music Corporation
Presser Place
Bryn Mawr, Pennsylvania 19010

Merion Music
Presser Place
Bryn Mawr, Pennsylvania 19010

Music Press, Inc.
P.O. Box 1052
Tuskegee Institute
Tuskegee, Alabama 36088

Neil Kjos Music Co.
4382 Jutland Drive
San Diego, California 92117

Novello and Co., Ltd.
145 Palisade Street
Dobbs Ferry, N.Y. 10522

Oxford University Press
200 Madison Avenue
New York, N.Y. 10016

Peer International Corp.
c/o Southern Music Co.
1740 Broadway
New York, N.Y. 10019

Peters, C. F.
373 Park Avenue South
New York, N.Y. 10016

Ricordi and Co.
c/o Belwin-Mills
25 Deshon Drive
Melville, N.Y. 11746

Robert King Music Co.
112 A Main Street
North Easton, Massachusetts 02356

Salabert Editions
c/oBelwin-Mills
25 Deshon Drive
Melville, N.Y. 11746

Sam Fox Publishing Co.
62 Cooper Square
New York, N.Y. 10003

Schmitt, Hall & McCreary
110 North Fifth Street
Minneapolis, Minnesota 55415

Shawnee Press, Inc.
Delaware Water Gap,
Pennsylvania 18327

Southern Music Publishing Co.
1740 Broadway
New York, N.Y. 10019

Spratt Music Publishers
c/o Plymouth Music Co.
8th Floor
17 West 60th Street
New York, N.Y. 10023

Stainer & Bell
c/o Galaxy Music Corp.
2121 Broadway
New York, N.Y. 10023

Theodore Presser Company
Presser Place
Bryn Mawr, Pennsylvania 19010

Walton Music Corp.
c/o Plymouth Music Co.
8th Floor
17 West 60th Street
New York, N.Y. 10023

World Library of Sacred Music
2145 Central Parkway
Cincinnati, Ohio 45214

Appendix III

A Selected List of Choral Music

The following list of choral music does not duplicate compositions included in Chapter 2; this list is limited to short, published choral compositions. Rental music may be obtained from the publisher, or from the rental libraries listed in Chapter 1.

THE MIXED CHOIR

A Babe Is Born – Daniel Moe; Theo. Presser; SATB; 312-40254

A Choral Flourish – R. Vaughan Williams; Oxford Univ.; SATB; 43.934

A Christmas Carol – N. Dello Joio; E.B. Marks; SATB; 4237

A Jazz Alleluia – Noël Goemanne; Mark Foster; Mixed Choir; MF 139

Ad te Domine – Kenneth Gaburo; World Library of Sacred Music; SATB

Adoramus te – Jacques Clement; Mercury Music; SATB; 352-00126

Adoramus te – W.A. Mozart; Oliver Ditson; SATB; 332-14445

Adoramus te – Palestrina; G. Schirmer; SATB

Adoramus te, Jesu Christe – Jacob Handl; Concordia; SATB-SATB; 98-2256

Adoration – Wm. Billings ed. Colvin; Elkan-Vogel; SATB; 362-03183

All Creatures Now Are Merry Minded – John Bennett; Stainer & Bell; SSATB

Alla riva del Tebro – Palestrina; E.C. Schirmer; SATB; 1147

Alleluia– Randall Thompson; E.C. Schirmer; SATB; 1786

Alleluia, I Heard a Voice – Thomas Weelkes; Oxford Univ.; SATBB; TMC 45

Also Hat Gitt Die Welt Geliebt – Heinrich Schütz; Sam Fox; SATBB; CM 7 (For God So Loved the World)

Am Bodensee – Robert Schumann; E.B. Marks; SATB; 37 (At the Lake of Constance)

Angelus ad Pastores Ait – Hans Leo Hassler; Assoc. Music Pub.; SATB; A 405

Anima mia Perdona – Claudio Monteverdi ed. Malin; Belwin-Mills; (Within my soul forgiveness) SSATB; Oct.2380

Ascendente Jesu in naviculam – Melchoir Vulpius; Concordia; SSATTB; Ms-1027

Assumpta est Maria – Palestrina ed. Boepple; Mercury Music; SSATTB; 352-00001

Ave Maria – Franz Liszt ed. Kaplin; Joseph Boonin; SATB; B.160

Ave Maria – W.A. Mozart; Arista; SATB; AE 106

Ave Maria – Giuseppe Verdi; E.B. Marks; SATB; 12588-4

Ave maris stella – Josquin des Prez; Assoc. Music Pub.; SATB; NYPM 35-21

Ave regina coelorum – Orlandus Lassus; Assoc. Music Pub.; SATB; 406

Ave Verum Corpus – Wm. Byrd; Assoc. Music Pub.; SATB; NYPMA 7-7

Be With Us at Our Table Lord – Gerhard Track; Augsburg Pub.; SATB; 11-1865

Behold Man – Ron Nelson; Boosey & Hawkes; SATB; 5972

Benedictus – G. Gabrieli ed. McKelvy; Mark Foster; SATB-TBBB; MF 411

Blessed be the Lord God of Israel – Thomas Tallis ed. Simpson; Concordia Pub.; SATB; 98-2277

Cantate Domino – Giovanni Croce; Arista; SATB; AE 199

Cantate Domino – Hans Leo Hassler ed. Ehret; Southern Music Pub., SSATB; 1057-11

Carols of Death – Wm Schuman; Merion Music; Mixed Chorus
   1. The Last Invocation 342-40011
   2. The Unknown Region 342-40012
   3. To All, To Each 342-40013

Chief Seattle's Psalm – Daniel Moe; Carl Fischer; SATB and Trumpet; CM 7995

Christe eleison – Francesco Durante; Colombo; SATB; NY 2003

Christus Factus Est – Anton Bruckner; C.F. Peters; SSAATTBB; 6316

Circles – Marcel Couraud; Mark Foster; SATB; MF 341 A

Circus Band – Charles Ives arr. Dashnaw; Peer International; SSATTBB; 2262-10

Come Again, Sweet Love – John Dowland; E.C. Schirmer; SATB

Come, All Musicians, Come – Hans Leo Hassler; G. Schirmer; SSATBB; 12032

Comfort All Ye My People – Fauré arr. Hopson; Carl Fischer; SATB; CM 8017

Cradle Song At Bethlehem – Arthur Pritchard; C.C. Birchard; SATB; 1230

Criste, Qui Lux Es Et Dies – Johann Walther; Concordia Pub.; SAATTB; MS-1030

Crossing the Bar – Charles Ives ed. Kirkpatrick; Assoc. Music Pub.; SATB;
A-702

Das Gelaur zu Speier – Ludwig Senfl; Bourne; SATTBB; ES 83
(The Bells of Speyer)

Das Ist Mir Lieb – Heinrich Schütz; Hänssler Verlag; SSATB
(Psalm 216)

Das Schiffen – Robert Schumann; A. Broude; SATB, Flute & Horn; 135
(A Lonely Boat Drifts Slowly)

Deo Gratias – Anonymous, Oxford Univ.; ATB or TTB

Der Abend, Op. 64, No. 2 – J. Brahms; G. Schirmer; SATB; 42948

Der Sänger – Robert Schumann; Assoc. Music Pub.; SATB; A 385-5
(The Singer)

Deus Misereature Nostri – Heinrich Schütz; Schmitt, Hall & McCreary;
(Oh Lord, Have Mercy Upon Us) SATB; 1401

Die Primel – F. Mendelssohn; Assoc. Music Pub.; SATB; A-382
(The Primrose)

Die Mit Tränen Säen – Johann Schein; Bourne; SSATB; 3022-12
(They Who Grieving Soweth)

Die Mit Tränen Säen – Heinrich Schütz; H. Flammer; SSATB; 84765
(They Who Grieving Soweth)

Dixit Dominus – W.A. Mozart; Lawson-Gould; SATB; 51164
(Psalm 110)

Drei Volkslieder – F. Mendelssohn; European-American; SATB; EA 413

Easter Carol – Charles Ives; Assoc. Music Pub.; Solo Quartet, SATB &
Organ; A-684

Ecce Quomodo Moritur Justus – Palestrina; Ricordi; SATB & SSA; 1180-3

Eclatante Trompette – Jean-Philippe Rameau ed. Couraud; Mark Foster;
(Sound the Trumpet on High) SATB; MF 343

Ein Kindelein So Löbelich – M. Praetorius; Bärenreiter Verlag; SATB-
SATB; 2903

Es Geht Ein Wehen Durch Den Wald, Op. 62, No. 6 – J. Brahms; Assoc.
Music Pub.; SATBB; A 397

Es Ist Das Heil Uns Kommen Her – Hugo Distler ed. Richter; Joseph
(Now Has Salvation Come to Us), Boonin; SATB; B.293

Exultate Deo – Palestrina; G. Schirmer; SSATB; 7672

Exultate Deo – A. Scarlatti; Theo. Presser; SATB; 312-40166

Fa Una Canzone – Orazio Vecchi; Lawson-Gould; SATB; 556

Factus est Dominus – Orlandus Lassus; Concordia Pub.; SATB; 98-1742
(God is my Strong Defense)

Fantasia on Chrismas Carols – R. Vaughan Williams; Stainer & Bell;
SATB; 1223

Father of All – Christopher Tye; Novello; SATB; 135

Four Cummings Choruses – Vincent Persichetti; Elkan-Vogel;
    1. dominic has a doll 1222
    2. nouns to nouns 1223
    3. maggie and milly and molly and may 1224
    4. uncles 1225

Four Folk Songs – J. Brahms ed. Kaplan; Mercury Music; SATB; 352-
00435

Four Motets – Tomas Luis de Victoria; Assoc. Music Pub.; SATB; A 661
    1. Jesu dulcis memoria
    2. O quam gloriosum
    3. O! Domine (SAATTB)
    4. Vere Languores

Four Psalms – Heinrich Schütz; Mercury Music; SATB; 352-00006

Frau Musica – Paul Hindemith; Assoc. Music Pub.; High & Low Voices &
Mixed Instruments; 194437

Gloria in Excelsis Deo – Tomas Luis de Victoria ed. McKelvy; Mark Foster; SATB-SATB; MF 404

Gloria Patri – Thomas Tallis; Novello; SATB; TM 7

Glory to God – Ron Nelson; Boosey & Hawkes; SATB; 5321

Go, Lovely Rose – Halsey Stevens; Mark Foster; SATB; EH-1

Go Not Far From Me, O God – N.A. Zingarelli; H.W. Gray; SATB; 1464

God Is My Strong Salvation – Halsey Stevens; Mark Foster; SATB; MF
118

Gradual – Anton Bruckner ed. May; G. Schirmer; SATB; 12051

Haec Est Dies – Jacobus Gallus (Handl); Concordia Pub.; Double Chorus,
(This is the Day) or SATB & Brass; 98-1702

Haste Thee Nymph –G.F. Handel; C. Fischer; SATB; CM 6297

He Hath Done All Things Well – Jan Bender; Concordia Pub.; SATB;
98-1067

He Hermite – Anonymous; E.C. Schirmer; SATB; 2461
(Hey There, Mister)

He, Watching Over Israel – F. Mendelssohn; Oliver Ditson; SATB; 232-
00827

Hear My Prayer – F. Mendelssohn; Theo. Presser; SATB; 232-00827

Hear The Prayer We Raise – Henry Purcell arr. Stroud; Mark Foster; SATB; MF 101

Herz Lieb Zu Dir Allein – Hans Leo Hassler ed. Ehret; Boston Music Co.; (O, Dearest Love of Mine) SSATB; 13703

Hodie Christus Natus Est – Luca Marenzio; Concordia Pub.; SATB; 98-1810

Hodie Christus Natus Est – Francis Poulenc; Salabert/Colombo; SATB; SAL. 15

Hodie Christus Natus Est – Jan Pieters Sweelinck; E.B. Marks; SSATB; 4301

Hosanna to the Son of David – Leslie Adams; Walton Music; SATB; 2927

Hosanna to the Son of David – Orlando Gibbons; B.F. Wood; Mixed Chorus; 242

Hosanna to the Son of David – Thomas Weelkes; Oxford univ.; SSATBB; TCM-9

How Beautiful Upon The Mountains – Daniel Moe; Theo. Presser; SAB; 312-40230

How Lovely Is Thy Dwelling Place – J. Brahms; Oliver Ditson; SATB; 332-14704

Hungarian Folksongs – arr. Halsey Stevens; Mark Foster; SATB; MF 316

I Sing Of Your Mercies – Norwegien Folk Tune arr. Sateren; Augsburg Pub.; Mixed Choir; 11-1889

I Wrestle and Pray – J.C. Bach; H.W. Gray; SATB-SATB; CMR 1535

If I Got A Ticket, Can I Ride – arr. Shaw-Parker; Lawson-Gould; SATB; 9852

In Autumn – J. Brahms; G. Schirmer; SATB; 11416

In Dulci Jubilo – Dietrich Buxtehude; Concordia Pub.; SAB & Strings; 98-1500

In Dulci Jubilo – Samuel Scheidt; Bärenreiter Verlag; SSAT-ATBB, 2 Flutes or Violins; 692

In Monte Oliveti – Palestrina; Schmitt, Hall & McCreary; SATB; 1660

In Resurrectione Tua, Christe – Jakob Handl; Concordia Pub.; Double (In Thy Resurrection, Jesus Christ) Choir or SATB & Brass; 98-2258

Innsbruck, I Now Must Leave Thee – Heinrich Isaac; Carl Fischer; SATB; CM 7404

It Is Good To Be Merry – J. Brahms; Neil Kjos; SATB; 5293

Jauchzet, dem Herrn – Johann Pachelbel; Bärenreiter Verlag; SATB-SATB; BA 2874

Jesu, Thou The Virgin-Born – Gustav Holst; Concordia Pub.; SATB; 98-2183

Joseph Lieber, Joseph Mein – Johann Walther; Assoc. Music Pub.; SATB; A 400

Just As The Tide Was Flowing – R. Vaughan Williams; Galaxy; SATB; CL 130

Kyrie, K. 341 – W.A. Mozart ed. Landon; G. Schirmer; SATB; 12067

Kyrie in D minor – J.S. Bach; G. Schirmer; SSATB; 40257

Laboravi Clamans – Jean-Philippe Rameau; Assoc. Music Pub.; SSATB; A 410

Lauda Sion – Tomas Luis de Victoria; A. Broude; SATB-SATB; ABC 21

Laudate Dominum – W.A. Mozart; Lawson-Gould; SATB; 51165 (Psalm 117)

Laudate Jehovam, Omnes Gentes – Georg P. Telemann; Concordia Pub.; (Psalm 117) SATB & Strings; 97-4838

Lebenslust – Franz Schubert; A. Broude; SATB (Joy of Living)

Let Down The Bars, O Death – Samuel Barber; G. Schirmer; SATB; 8907

Let My Prayer Come Up – Henry Purcell; B.F. Wood; SSATB; 355

Letters In The Sand – Alan Hovhaness; Assoc. Music Pub.; SATB & Trumpet; A 732

Lie Lightly Gentle Earth – Paul Chihara; Shawnee Pres; SATB; A 1193

Lo, How A Rose E'er Blooming – Michael Praetorius; Lawson-Gould; SATB; 730

Look Down, O Lord – Wm Byrd ed. Wulstan; A. Broude; AATB; ABC 14

Lord, Now Lettest Thou – Henry Purcell; E.B. Marks; SATB; 85

Magnificat – Dietrich Buxtehude ed. Ehret; Theo. Presser; SSATB & Strings; 312-40987

Magnificat in G – Marc-Antoine Charpentier; Concordia Pub.; SATB; 97-6343

Magnificat in D – Johann Pachelbel; Bärenreiter Verlag; SATB; 97-7612

Make a Joyful Noise – A. Donato; Neil Kjos; Unison; 6099

Man That Is Born Of A Woman – Henry Purcell; Stainer & Bell; SATB; SNB 5502

May The God Of Wit Inspire – Henry Purcell; Assoc. Music Pub.; SATB; A 409

Meine Seele Erhebt Den Herren – Heinrich Schütz; Hänssler Verlag; SATB

Misericordias Domini – Francesco Durante; G. Schirmer; SATB-SATB; 11563

Missa Brevis St. Joannis de Deo – F. J. Haydn; Arista; SATB & Strings

Modern Music – Wm Billings; Mercury Music; SATB; MC 88

My God Is A Rock – arr. Shaw-Parker; Lawson-Gould; SATB; 51107

Nachtens, Op. 122, No. 2 – J. Brahms; G. Schirmer; SATB; 10133

Nature's Way – Charles Ives trans. Haufrecht; Peer International; SATB; 2295-3

Nimmersatte Liebe – Hugo Distler ed. Richter; Bärenreiter Verlag; (Insatiable Love) SSATB; B 297

Nun Danket alla Gott – Johann Pachelbel; Robert King; SATB & Brass; 604

O Bone Jesu – P. Agostini; Bourne; SATB; ES 79

O Clap Your Hands – R. Vaughan Williams; Galaxy; SSAATTBB & Brass; 222

O How Amiable – Thomas Weelkes; Oxford Univ.; SAATB; TCM 90

O Jonathan – Thomas Weelkes; Assoc. Music Pub.; SSAATB; NYPMA 12

O Magnum Mysterium – Palestrina; Assoc. Music Pub.; SSAATB; A 526

O Magnum Mysterium – Francis Poulenc; Salabert/Columbo; SATB; Sal. 12

O Magnum Mysterium – Tomas Luis de Victoria; G. Schirmer; SATB; 10193

O Magnum Mysterium – Adrian Willaert; Arista; SATB; 217

O Mistress Mine – R. Vaughan Williams; SATB; Galaxy; 60092

O, My God, Bestow Thy Tender Mercy – G. Pergolesi arr. Hopson; Carl Fischer; Two-part treble and male; CM 7974

O Salutaris Hostia – Gioacchino Rossini; Broude; SATB; 127

O Schöne Nacht – J. Brahms ed. Klein; G. Schirmer; SATB; 11800 (O Lovely Night)

O Vos Omnes – Tomas Luis de Victoria; Arista; SATB; AE 162

Old Home Day – Charles Ives ed. Smith; Peer International; Unison

On Christmas Night – R. Vaughan Williams; Galaxy Music; Unison or SATB; 1.5130.1

Pater Noster – Palestrina, ed. Kraft; Mercury Music; SSATB; 352-00455
(The Lord's Prayer)

Pater Noster – Heiter Villa-Lobos; E.B. Marks; SATB; 12898-4
(The Lord's Prayer)

Petite Nymphe Folâtre – Clement Jannequin; Mark Foster; SATB; MF 303
(Frolicsome Nymph)

Prayer of St. Francis of Assisi – Ron Nelson; Boosey & Hawkes; SATB;
5930

Proverb – Vincent Persichetti; Elkan-Vogel; SATB; 1102

Psalm 23 – George Rochberg; Theo. Presser; SATB; 312-40297

Psalm 43 – George Rochberg; Theo. Presser; SSATBB; 312-40298

Psalm 66 – Hans Leo Hassler ed. McKelvy; Mark Foster; SSAT-ATBB; MF
402

Psalm 90 – Charles Ives; Merion Music; SATB, Organ & Bells; 342-40021

Psalm 100 – Heinrich Schütz; Bärenreiter Verlag; SATB-SATB; 480

Psalm 130 – H. Zimmerman; Carl Fischer; SATB; CM 8028

Psalm 150 – George Rochberg; Theo. Presser; SATB; 312-40299

Quaerite Primum Regnum Dei – W.A. Mozart ed. Smith; Mark Foster;
SATB; MF 157

Quand la meijonue sounavo – Nicholas Saboly; E.C. Schirmer; SATB; 2204
(The Hour of Midnight Sounded)

Quare Fremuerunt Gentes: Finale – Michel-Richard de La Lande ed.
Couraud; Mark Foster; SATBB; MF 174

Quem vidistis Pastores Dicite – Francis Poulenc; Salabert/Colombo; SATB;
Sal. 13

Regina Coeli – Antonio Caldara; Arista; SATB; AE 205

Regina Coeli – W.A. Mozart; G. Schirmer; SATB; 2306

Reincarnations – Samuel Barber; G. Schirmer; SATB
1. Mary Hynes 8908
2. Anthony O'Daly 8909
3. The Coolin 8910

Rejoice in the Lord Always – Henry Purcell; Bourne; SATB; ES 81

Resignation – Hugo Wolf; Boonin; SATB; 114

Rest – R. Vaughan Williams; Galaxy Music; SSATB; 1.2478.1

Salve O Vergine Maria – G. Rossini; Assoc. Music Pub.; SATB; A 411

Sancti Spiritus – Carlo Gesualdo; Ricordi; SATTB; NY 1908

Saul – Heinrich Schütz ed. Beyerle; C.F. Peters; SSATBB-SATB-SATB; 4815

Sea Charms – Frederick Piket; Assoc. Music Pub.; SATB; A 141

Senex Puerum Portabat – Tomas Luis de Victoria; Shawnee Press; SATB; A-135b

Sicut Cervus – Palestrina; Mercury Music; SATB; MP 75

Sicut Moses Serpentem – Heinrich Schütz; Assoc. Music Pub.; SATB; A-412

Sing Praise to Christ – J.S. Bach; Concordia Pub.; SATB; 98-1377

Sing to the Lord – Christopher Tye; Novello & Co.; SATB; 115

Singet dem Herrn ein neues Lied – Hugo Distler; Bärenreiter Verlag; Mixed Choir; 751

S'io fusse ciaul – Orlandus Lassus; G. Schirmer; SATB; 11960

Sommerlied, Op. 146, No. 4 – Robert Schumann; Sam Fox; SATB; RC 12

Songs of Nature, Op. 63 – Anton Dvorak; Broude; SATB; B 85

Stomp Your Foot – A. Copland; Boosey & Hawkes; SATB & 4-hand Piano; 5019

Stopping By Woods On A Snowy Evening – Ron Caviani; Mark Foster; SATB; MF 342

Stranger, Share Our Fire – Daniel Moe; Augsburg Pub.; SATB; 11-529

Surely He Hath Born Our Griefs – Karl H. Graun ed. Buszin; Concordia Pub.; SATB; 98-1171

Surgens Jesus – Peter Philips; Arista; SSATB; 196

Surrexit Pastor Bonus – Samuel Scheidt; Hänssler Verlag; SSAT-ATBB & Strings; 165

Te Deum – W.A. Mozart; Broude; SATB & Strings; 255

The Beatitudes – Franz Liszt; Arista; SSAATTBB; AE 176

The Best of Rooms – R. Thompson; E.C. Schirmer; SATB; 1265

The Cherry Tree Carol – arr. Shaw-Parker; G. Schirmer; SATB; 10170

The Dark Eyed Sailor – R. Vaughan Williams; Galaxy Music; SATB; 1.5097.1

The Dove's Message – Bohuslav Martinu; Boosey & Hawkes; SATB; 1843

The Gold Threaded Robe– Peter Mennin; Carl Fischer; SATB; 6418

The Jolly Tar and the Milkmaid – George Gershwin ed. Smith; Lawson-Gould: SATB; 51963

The Lamentations of Jeremiah (Part I) – Thomas Tallis; G. Schirmer; SATTB; 44185c

The Lord is a Mighty God – F. Mendelssohn; Neil Kjos; Two-part mixed voices; 9

The Old Hundredth Psalm Tune – R. Vaughan Williams; Oxford Univ.; SATB; 42953

The Road Not Taken – R. Thompson; E.C. Schirmer; SATB; 2485

The Springtime of the Year – R. Vaughan Williams; Galaxy; SATB; 129

The Ways of Zion Do Mourn – Michael Wise; E.C. Schirmer; SATB; 2680

The Willow Song – R. Vaughan Williams; Mills Music; SATB; 242

Three Choral Songs for Christmas – Michael Praetorious; Mercury; SATB; MC 244-15

Three Chorales – J.S. Bach; Bourne; SATB; WE 5
(from *Christmas Oratorio*)

Three Fuguing Tunes – Wm Billings; Mercury Music; SATB; 352-00361

Three Harvest Home Chorales – Charles Ives; Mercury Music; SATB; 351-00361

Three Hungarian Folksongs – B. Bartok; Boosey & Hawkes; SATB; 5326

Three Mixed Choruses – L. Janacek; European American; SATB; B 336, B 337, B 338

Three Tantum Ergos, Op. 45 – Franz Schubert; Arista; SATB; AE 177

Tibi Laus – Orlando di Lasso; Concordia Pub.; SATB; 98-2294
(Praise Be Thine)

Timor et Tremor – G. Gabrieli; Pennsylvania Univ. Press; Mixed Choir

To Us Is Born A Blessed Child – Daniel Moe; Augsburg; SATB; 1265

Today Is Born Emmanuel – M. Praetorius ed. Vree; Mark Foster; SATB; MF 510

Tota Pulchra – Anton Bruckner; Arista; SSAATTBB; AE 171

Touro – Louro – Louro! – Nicolas Saboly; Lawson-Gould; SSAATTBB; 10167

Tristis est Anima mea – Johann Kuhnau; Concordia Pub.; SSATB; 98-1971

Trois Chansons – Claude Debussy; Durand; SATB; D & F 7179

Two Motets – Claudio Monteverdi; Oxford Univ.; SSATTB; 43.345
    1. Adoramus Te
    2. Cantatae Domino

Two Madrigals by Michelangelo – Jacob Arcadelt; Marks; SATB; 12648-9

Twenty-Four Canons – F. Haydn; C.F. Peters; SATB; 6999

Unser Seele Wartet Auf Den Herrn – John Antes; Boosey & Hawkes;
(Our Soul Doth Wait Upon The Lord) SATB; 5941

Ve Drassi Prima Sensa Luce Il Sole – Palestrina; Bourne; SATB; ES 61

Verbum Caro Factum Est – Hans Leo Hassler ed. Wilhelm; Mark Foster;
(God Now Dwells Among Us) SAB or TBB; MF 129

Victimae Paschali Laudes – Tomas Luis de Victoria; Schmitt, Hall &
   McCreary; SATB; 1412

Videntes Stellam – Francis Poulenc; Salabert/Colombo; SATB; Sal. 14

Vom Himmel Hoch – Johann Schien; Marks; SSATB; 4293
(From Heaven Above To Earth I Come)

Waltz – Charles Ives ed. Smith; Peer International; SATB

We Turn Our Eyes To Thee – M. Praetorius; Belwin-Mills; SATB-SATB;
   2268

When David Heard That Absalom Was Slain – Thomas Tomkins; G.
   Schirmer; SSATB; 11287

When Shall My Sorrowful Sighing? – Thomas Tallis; Oxford Univ.; SATB;
   351

Wie Schön Leuchtet Der Morgenstern – M. Praetorius ed. Beyerle; C.F.
   Peters; SATB-SSTTB; 4806

You Are The Way – arr. Sateren; Augsburg Pub.; SATB; 11-0553

Young Cupid Hath Proclaimed – Thomas Weelkes; Assoc. Music Pub.;
   SATB; A-413

Your Lovely Face – Hans Leo Hassler ed. Gronquist; A. Broude; SATB;
   AB 741

THE FEMALE CHOIR

Ach Gott, Vom Himmel Sieh Darein – Hugo Distler; European-American;
(Oh God, From Heaven Look On Us) SSA; EA 405

Ave Maria – Zoltan Kodaly; Boosey & Hawkes; SSAA

Don't Leave Me – B. Bartok; Boosey & Hawkes; SA; 1668

Five Canzonets – Daniel Pinkham; Assoc. Music Pub.; SA

Four Russian Peasant Songs – Igor Stravinsky; E.B. Marks; SSAA

French Chansons – ed. H. David; Mercury Music; SS or SA; MC 54

How Excellent Thy Name – Howard Hanson; C. Fischer; SSAA; CM 6706

Lift Thine Eyes – F. Mendelssohn; Oliver Ditson; SSA; 332-00820

Now I Lay Me Down To Sleep – R. Thompson; E.C. Schirmer; SSA; 1985

O Lady Moon – Alan Hovhaness; E.B. Marks; SSA & Clarinet; MC 4653

O Primavera – Felice Anerio; Belwin-Mills; SSA; Oct. 2377
(O Lovely Springtime)

Simple Gifts – Aaron Copland; Boosey & Hawkes; SA; 1903

Sing Joyfully – Alec Wyton; Mercury Music; Treble Voices; MC 457

The Gate of Heaven – R. Thompson; E.C. Schirmer; SSAA; 2531

Three Sacred Choruses – J. Brahms; C.F. Peters; SSAA; 66141

To Be Sung On The Water – Samuel Barber; G. Schirmer; Treble Voices;
   11826

Wir Glauben An Gott, Den Vater – Hugo Distler; Bärenreiter Verlag; SSA;
   EA 404

THE MALE CHOIR

Behold Man – Ron Nelson; Boosey & Hawkes; Male Voices; 5403

Brothers, Lift Your Voices – L. Pfautsch; H.W. Gray; TTBB; CMR 2556

Carnival Song – Walter Piston; Assoc. Music Pub.; Male Voices; A-296

Catches For Men's Voices – Henry Purcell; Oxford Univ.; Equal Voices

Clap Your Hands, Stomp Your Feet – Ron Nelson; Augsburg Pub.; Male
   Voices; 11-0649

I Feel Death – Ned Rorem; Boosey & Hawkes; TBB; 5624

In That New Jerusalem – arr. DeCormier; Lawson-Gould; TTBB; 51091

Jaglied – F. Mendelssohn; G. Schirmer; TTBB; 12074
(Hunting Song)

Mary Had A Baby – arr. Shaw-Parker; Lawson-Gould; TTBB; 10191

O Lord, In Thee Is All My Trust – T. Tallis; Concordia Pub.; TTBB;
   98-1684

O Sing Unto The Lord – N. Dello Joio; C. Fischer; TTBB; CM 7138

Poor Man Lazarus – arr. J. Hairston; Bourne; TTBB; S 1022

Sailor's Farewell – Henry Purcell; Summy-Birchard; TTBB; 5718

Song Of Peace – V. Persichetti; Elkan-Vogel; Male Voices; 130

Stopping By Woods – R. Thompson; E.C. Schirmer; TTBB; 2182

Trinklied – F. Mendelssohn ed. Mueller; G. Schirmer; TTBB; 12034
(Drinking Song)

THE CHAMBER CHOIR

A Che Tormi il ben mio – Claudio Monteverdi; G. Schirmer; SSATB; 51153

Adieu, Sweet Amarillis – John Wilbye; Walton Music; SATB; 7000

April Is In My Mistress' Face – Thomas Morley; E. C. Schirmer; SATB

As On The Night Before This Blessed Morn – Orlando Gibbons; Concordia; SATB; 98-1756

Ave Maria – Jean Mouton; Music Press; SATB; DCS 40

Vaci, Soavi e Cari – Claudio Monteverdi; Boston Music; SSATB; 13704
(Kisses, So Sweet and Burning)

Bonjour, mon Coeur – Orlandus Lassus; E.C. Schirmer; SATB; 416

Ce mois de may – Clement Jannequin; Salabert; SATB; 3029

Chanson – Orlandus Lassus; G. Schirmer; SATB; 7127

Ego Sum Panis Vivus – Wm. Byrd; A. Broude; SATB; ABC 30

Einklang – Hugo Wolf; Boonin; SATB; 113
(Harmony)

Fair Phyllis I Saw – John Farmer; Harold Flammer; SATB; 3258

Hark All Ye Lovely Saints – Thomas Weelkes; Stainer & Bell; SSATB; 1488

I Weep Now – L. Marenzio; C. Fischer; SATB; CM 7559

Il et bel et bon – Passereau; Salabert; Mixed Choir; 3075

Il S'en Va Tard – Clement Jannequin; Broude; SATB; 143
(A Storm Has Brewed)

It Was A Lover And His Lass – Thomas Morley; H.W. Gray; SATB; 553

Last Night I Dreamed – Max Reger; Marks; SATB; 60

Ma per me lasso – Luca Marenzio; Marks; SATB; 4326
(Ah, Weary Am I)

Madrigal – Carlo Gesualdo; Marks; SSATB; 12995

Marie – Francis Poulenc; Durand and Co.; SATB; D & F 12691

Now Is The Month Of Maying – T. Morley; Bourne; SATB; ES 75

O Bella Fusa – Orlandus Lassus; G. Schirmer; SATB; 11338
(The Spinning Wheel)

O Quantus luctus hominum – Palestrina; Assoc. Music Pub.; SATB; A 408

O Sacrum Convivium – Wm. Byrd; Arista; SATB; AE 192

O Sacrum Convivium – Olivier Messiaen; Durand & Co.; SATB; D & F 12742

O Softly Singing Lute – Francis Pilkington; Choral Art; SSAATB; 5103

On The Plains, Fairy Trains – Thomas Weelkes ed. Deller; G. Schirmer; SSATB; 12044

Quand mon mari – Orlandus Lassus; Walton; SATB; 8013

Scherzi Musicali – Claudio Monteverdi; Bärenreiter Verlag; SSB & Strings

See, See The Shepherds' Queen – Thomas Tomkins ed. Deller; G. Schirmer; SSATB; 12046

Some Men Desire Spouses – Thomas Weelkes; Stainer & Bell; SSA or ATB; 1792

Ten Provencal Carols – Nicolas Saboly; H.W. Gray; SATB

Three Shakespearean Songs – R. Vaughan Williams; Oxford Univ.; SATB; 53.033

Wer Will Uns Scheiden – Heinrich Schütz; Sam Fox; SATB; CM 11 (Who Shall Separate Us?)

When David Heard – Thomas Weelkes; Assoc. Music Pub.; SSAATB; NYMPA 11

CHORAL MUSIC WITH ELECTRONIC TAPE

A Child's Ghetto – Hanley Jackson; Walton Music; SATB & Tape; 2916

A Time For Every Purpose – Gilbert Trythall; E.B. Marks; 4495

Collect – Leslie Bassett; World Library; SATB & Tape; CA 2000-8

Cosmic Festival – Richard Felciano; E.C. Schirmer; Unison Voices & Tape; 2938

Cradle Hymn and Hodie – Hanley Jackson; Shawnee; A 1319

Digressions – Barry Vercoe; Elkan-Vogel; Double Choir, Tape, Winds, Strings, and Percussion

Festive Psalm – Brian Fennelly; American Composers Alliance; Choir, Tape, Narrator, & Organ

Hands Full – Doris Hays; A. Broude; Two-part Chorus, Tape, and Bongos

Hymn of the Universe – Richard Felciano; E.C. Schirmer; SAB & Tape; 2944

I Will Lift Up Mine Eyes – Don Muro; H.W. Gray; CCS 25

In The Beginning of Creation – Daniel Pinkham; E.C. Schirmer; 2902

Kyrie – Donald Erb; Marion Music; 342-40026

Passacaglia – Johan France; American Composers Alliance

Pentecost Sunday – Richard Felciano; World Library; Unison Male Voices, (Double Alleluia) Organ & Tape; EMP 1532-1

Psalm XIII – Karl Korte; E.C. Schirmer

Quodlibet For Singers – Barney Childs; American Composers Alliance; Mixed Chorus & Tape

Rituals and Reactions – Elias Tanenbaum; American Composers Alliance; Choir, Tape, 5-Brass, and Percussion

Signs – Richard Felciano; E.C. Schirmer; SATB; Choir, Tape & Porjectors; 2927

Spirits of the Dead – Dwight Gatwood; A. Broude; TTBB and Tape

Still Are New Worlds – Ross Lee Finney; Choir, Tape, Narrator, and Orchestra

Synchronism #4 – Mario Davidovsky; E.B. Marks
(Psalm 70)

Tangents V – Hanley Jackson; Shawnee Press; SATB & Tape; 2916

The Not-Yet Flower – Richard Felciano; E.C. Schirmer; Unison Voices and (A Crisis For Growth) Tape; 2937

The Sheepheards Song – Daniel Pinkham; E.C. Schirmer; SATB & Optional Tape; 2913

Three Chinese Poems – Robert Stern; J. Boonin; Double Treble Choir, Tape, Viola, Piano, Celeste, & Percussion

Three-In-One-In-Three – Richard Felciano; E.C. Schirmer; SAB-SAB, optional Organ & other instruments; 2910

Three Scenes From The Creation – Vladimir Ussachevsky; American Composers Alliance
  1. Prologue
  2. Interlude
  3. Epilogue

Variations – Barney Childs; American Composers Alliance; Mixed Choir Tape, and Bells

Words of St. Peter – Richard Felciano; World Library; SATB, Organ, & Tape; CA-2093-8

Selected Bibliography

Ades, Hawley. *Choral Arranging*. Delaware Water Gap, Pa.: Shawnee Press, 1968.

Aldrich, Putnam. *The Principle Agréments of the 17th and 18th Centuries: A Study in Musical Ornamentation*. Cambridge Mass.: Harvard University Press, 1942.

Arnold, Franck T. *The Art of Accompaniment from a Thorough-Bass*. 2 vols. New York: Dover Publications, 1965.

Boult, Adrian Cedric, and Emery, Walter. *The St. Matthew Passion: Its Preparation and Performance*. London: Novello, 1949.

Boyd, Jack. *Rehearsal Guide For The Choral Director*. West Nyack, N. Y.: Parker Publishing Company, 1970.

Brown, Howard M. *Embellishing 16th-Century Music*. London: Oxford University Press, 1976.

Cone, Edward T. *Musical Form and Musical Performance*. N. Y.: W. W. Norton and Co., 1968.

Dannreuther, Edward. *Musical Ornamentation*. 2 vols. London: Novello, n.d.

Dart, Thurston. *The Interpretation of Music*. Harper Colophon Books. New York: Harper & Row, 1963.

Davison, Archibald T. *The Technique of Choral Composition*. Cambridge, Mass.: Harvard University Press, 1945.

Decker, Harold, and Herford, Julius, (eds.). *Choral Conducting: A Symposium*. Englewood Cliffs, N. J.: Prentice-Hall, Inc., 1973.

Dolmetsch, Arnold. *The Interpretation of the Music of the XVIIth and XVIIIth Centuries*. London: Novello, 1946.

Dorian, Frederick. *The History of Music in Performance: The Art of Musical Interpretation from the Renaissance to Our Day*. New York: W. W. Norton and Co., 1966.

Ehmann, Wilhelm. *Choral Directing*. Trans. by George Wiebe. Minneapolis, Minn.: Augsburg, 1968.

Fellows, Edmund Horace. *The English Madrigal Composers*. 2nd. ed. London: Oxford University Press, 1948.

Fuhr, Hayes M. *Fundamentals of Choral Expression*. Lincoln, Nebr.: University of Nebraska Press, 1944.

Jacobs, Arthur, (ed.). *Choral Music: A Symposium.* Baltimore: Penguin Books, 1963.

Jipson, Wayne R. *The High School Vocal Music Program.* West Nyack, N. Y.: Parker Publishing Company, 1972.

Kerr, Anita. *Voices.* N.Y.: MCA Music, 1972.

Marshall, Madeleine. *The Singer's Manual of English Diction.* New York: G. Schirmer, 1953.

McElheran, Brock. *Conducting Technique for Beginners and Professionals.* New York: Oxford University Press, 1966.

Moe, Daniel. *Basic Choral Concepts.* Minneapolis, Minn.: Augsburg, 1972.

Pooler, Frank, and Pierce, Brent. *New Choral Notation.* New York: Walton Music Corp, 1971.

Robinson, Ray, (ed.). *Choral Music.* New York: W. W. Norton and Co., 1978.

Schreiber, Flora R., and Persichetti, Vincent. *William Schuman.* New York: G. Schirmer, Inc., 1954.

Schünemann, Georg. *Geschichte des Dirigens.* Leipzig: Breitkopf und Härtel, 1913.

Shaw, Watkins. *A Textual and Historical Companion to Handel's "Messiah."* London: Novello, 1965.

Smallman, Basil. *The Background of Passion Music: J. S. Bach and His Predecessors.* S. C. M. Press, 1957.

Stevens, Denis. *Tudor Church Music.* 2nd. ed. London: Faber and Faber, 1966.

Stevenson, Robert. *Protestant Church Music in America.* New York: W. W. Norton and Co., 1966.

Terry, Charles Sanford. *Bach: The Mass in B Minor.* 2nd. ed. London: Oxford University Press, 1958.

Tovey, Donald Francis. *Essays in Musical Analysis, Vol. V: Vocal Music.* London: Oxford University Press, 1956.

Ulrich, Homer. *A Survey of Choral Music.* New York: Harcourt Brace Jovanovich, Inc., 1973.

Werner, Eric. *In the Choir Loft: A Manual For Organists and Choir Directors in American Synagogues.* New York: Union of American Hebrew Congregations, 1957.

Werner, Jack. *Mendelssohn's "Elijah": A Historical and Analytical Guide to the Oratorio.* London: Chappell, 1965.

Whittaker, W. Gillies. *The Cantatas of Johann Sebastian Bach.* 2 vols. London: Oxford University Press, 1959.

Wienandt, Elwyn A. *Choral Music of the Church.* New York: Free Press, 1965.

Young, Percy M. *The Choral Tradition.* New York: W. W. Norton and Co., 1971.

Index

NOTE: ALL ENTRIES IN
BOLD TYPE ARE TITLES OF
MUSICAL COMPOSITIONS